An Introduction to Capitalism

AN INTRODUCTION TO CAPITALISM

EAMONN BUTLER

Institute of
Economic Affairs

First published in Great Britain in 2018 by
The Institute of Economic Affairs
2 Lord North Street
Westminster
London SW1P 3LB
in association with London Publishing Partnership Ltd
www.londonpublishingpartnership.co.uk

The mission of the Institute of Economic Affairs is to improve understanding of the fundamental institutions of a free society by analysing and expounding the role of markets in solving economic and social problems.

A CIP catalogue record for this book is available from the British Library.

ISBN 978-0-255-36758-5

Many IEA publications are translated into languages other than English or are reprinted. Permission to translate or to reprint should be sought from the Director General at the address above.

Typeset in Kepler by T&T Productions Ltd
www.tandtproductions.com

Printed and bound in Great Britain by Page Bros Ltd.

CONTENTS

The author   ix

1   Introduction   1

What this book is about   1
What the book covers   1
Who the book is for   2
Capitalism and the author   3
How this book is structured   3

2   What capitalism is   5

Reality and misconceptions   5
The disparagement of capitalism   6
The problems of definition   8
Wider associations of capitalism   9
Things not essential to capitalism   10
Things not unique to capitalism   11
Defining capitalism   14

3   What capital is   16

The concept of capital   16
The purpose of capital   16
How capital boosts productivity   17

Traditional notions of capital 19

The most important form of capital 21

Systems infrastructure 23

Legal and cultural capital 25

Conclusion 27

4 How capital is created 28

Mistaken ideas about capital acquisition 28

Capital is not easy to keep 30

Capital depends on human valuation 35

The real origin of capital 36

Capital versus coercion 37

5 Why the capital structure is crucial 39

The network of productive goods 40

The fragility of the capital structure 41

Bad policy kills capital 44

Conclusion 46

6 What makes capitalism work 48

Self-interest, property, profit and incentives 48

The process of competition 54

Specialisation and markets 55

Capitalism and the state 58

7 The moral dimension of capitalism 60

The socialist and capitalist moral vision 60

Capitalism creates value and spreads wealth 61

The human benefits of property rights 63

Equality and prosperity 65

The problem of defining equality 66

Capitalism improves human relations 68

Comparing like with like 69

8 The short history of capitalism 71

Twisting capitalism to fit the theory 71

State-directed commerce 72

The Industrial Revolution 74

The state-managed economy 76

The scourge of corporatism 78

Creating a capitalism for the future 80

9 Great thinkers on capitalism 82

The School of Salamanca (the 'Scholastics') 82

Adam Smith (1723–90) 83

David Ricardo (1772–1823) 85

Ludwig von Mises (1881–1973) 86

F. A. Hayek (1899–1992) 87

Milton Friedman (1912–2006) 88

James M. Buchanan (1919–2013) and Gordon Tullock (1922–2014) 89

Gary Becker (1930–2014) 91

Israel Kirzner (1930–) 92

Deirdre McCloskey (1942–) 93

10 Critics and criticisms 95

Moral criticisms 96

Structual criticisms 100

Corporate power 103
Global relationships 104
Confounding the cronies 106

11 The future of capitalism 108
Strengths 108
Weaknesses 110
Opportunities 113
Threats 115
The durability of capitalism 118

12 Further reading 119
Hostile introductions 119
Sympathetic introductions 120
On capitalism and poverty 123
On philosophy and morality 124

About the IEA 126

THE AUTHOR

Eamonn Butler is Director of the Adam Smith Institute, one of the world's leading policy think tanks. He holds degrees in economics and psychology, a PhD in philosophy, and an honorary DLitt. In the 1970s he worked in Washington for the US House of Representatives, and taught philosophy at Hillsdale College, Michigan, before returning to the UK to help found the Adam Smith Institute. A former winner of the Freedom Medal awarded by Freedom's Foundation of Valley Forge and the UK National Free Enterprise Award, Eamonn is currently Secretary of the Mont Pelerin Society.

Eamonn is author of many books, including introductions to the pioneering economists and thinkers Adam Smith, Milton Friedman, F. A. Hayek, Ludwig von Mises and Ayn Rand. He has also published primers on classical liberalism, public choice, Magna Carta, the Austrian School of Economics and great liberal thinkers, as well as *The Condensed Wealth of Nations* and *The Best Book on the Market*. His *Foundations of a Free Society* won the 2014 Fisher Prize. He is co-author of *Forty Centuries of Wage and Price Controls*, and of a series of books on IQ. He is a frequent contributor to print, broadcast and online media.

1   INTRODUCTION

What this book is about

It is hard to find a book that explains, simply and fairly, what capitalism is, how it works, and its strengths and weaknesses.

The very word *capitalism* was coined as a term of abuse. And still today, most books on the subject remain hostile to capitalism, or paint a distorted, confused picture of it. So commonplace is this that even capitalism's own supporters have trouble understanding what it is, and find themselves struggling to excuse the distortion rather than explain the reality.

There is, therefore, need for a short guide that outlines the subject of capitalism plainly and fairly. This is that book.

What the book covers

The book cuts through the prejudice and distortion to come up with a better definition of what capitalism actually is – and, just as importantly, what it is *not* – stripping away the clutter that critics have loaded onto it, so that the core essence of capitalism can be understood.

It also identifies what *capital* is, what forms it takes, how and why it comes into existence, its purpose, its use and its effects. It explores the *economic, social* and *moral* nature of capitalism and the institutions that uphold it.

The book traces the history of capitalism, explains some of the key ideas of those who support it, and reviews the criticisms of those who do not. And it provides a frank assessment of capitalism's strengths and weaknesses, and of its future.

Who the book is for

This book is written in plain, straightforward language, free of the jargon, the technical terms, the footnotes and glossaries of academic tomes. Its aim is to allow *anyone* to understand what capitalism is really about – and to help those who think they understand capitalism to understand it better.

The book should certainly help school and college students towards such a better understanding – and, since the majority of college teachers remain hostile to capitalism, suggest some sharp questions that students may test them with.

But it is also accessible to lay persons, including businesspeople, politicians and ordinary members of the public who are interested in economic and political ideas, and seek a straightforward guide through the ideas and arguments.

Capitalism and the author

Few authors on capitalism state their prejudices, or even realise they have them. So they draw readers into their own misconceptions and leave them thinking that those views are objective.

I happily admit that I support the ideal of capitalism – though not always the reality. I reject the idea that capitalism is fundamentally immoral and antisocial. Rather, I believe that capitalism is severely distorted by the interventions of politicians and then blamed, unfairly, for the consequences. But even in this distorted state, capitalism has still spread prosperity across the planet.

So I remain sympathetic to the ideal of capitalism, but mindful of the criticisms made of both the concept and the reality. In answering these criticisms here, I hope to do no more than to rebalance the debate and leave the reader with a fair explanation of what capitalism really is.

How this book is structured

The book starts by trying to identify what capitalism is – and is not. It then explains what capital is, where it comes from, what it does, why we need it, and the critical importance (often overlooked by critics and supporters alike) of how a community's capital is structured and intertwined.

It then examines the things that are needed to make capitalism work, exploring the role and nature of property, ownership, incentives, competition, markets, institutions and the state. Next, it considers the moral criticisms made of capitalism, along with its (more rarely heard) positive moral vision and effects.

The book then puts capitalism in its historical context, charting the economic systems that helped create the ideals and principles of capitalism and the political interventions that have so widely eclipsed and perverted them.

Next, the book explains briefly the ideas of some of the leading intellectual champions of capitalism, and addresses the criticisms of its detractors.

Last, it outlines capitalism's strengths, weaknesses, opportunities and threats, before assessing its future and leaving the reader with a brief list of further sources that bring more insight onto this fascinating subject.

2   WHAT CAPITALISM IS

Reality and misconceptions

However you define it, capitalism has brought a vast rise in human wealth and living standards. Until the dawn of the Industrial Revolution in the 1760s, human life changed little. Most people worked on the land, using methods that had changed little since the Pharaohs. In 1800, as the American economic historian Deirdre Mc-Closkey (1942–) calculates, the average world citizen's income was between $1 and $5 a day. Now it averages nearly $50 a day. And even that average masks the huge prosperity that the more capitalist countries have achieved. While some of today's most anti-capitalist countries remain mired in $1–5 a day poverty, average daily earnings in capitalist Switzerland, Australia, Canada and the UK now exceed $90 a day. US earnings average over $100 a day, making modern Americans 20–100 times richer than their ancestors in 1800.

Nor has this huge rise in prosperity been confined to a rich few. In the capitalist countries, things that were once luxuries – decent housing, sanitation, lighting and heating, spare clothes, travel, leisure, entertainment, fresh meat

– have become accessible to all. Machines now take the hard work out of industrial production and home chores. Health, child survival, longevity and education have all improved markedly.

The disparagement of capitalism

Yet even as this 'Great Enrichment' (as McCloskey calls it) unfolded, the word *capitalism* was being turned into a term of contempt. The root word *capital* goes back to the 1100s, where the Latin term *capitale* (from *caput*, meaning 'head') was used for stocks of cattle, and later, for goods or money; *capitalist*, meaning simply an owner of capital, appears in the 1600s. But by 1867, despite the enrichment that the Industrial Revolution had brought, the German political thinker Karl Marx (1818–83) was scorning the 'capitalist mode of production' – what today we call *capitalism* – in his book *Das Kapital*.

It was a hugely successful attack, for Marx's polemics still shape the debate today. Many people still regard capitalism as rooted in antisocial or immoral motives, such as selfishness, greed and a lack of concern for others. Often, capitalism is even defined in terms of such motives – with the presumption that no social good can ever come from them. Socialism, however, is regarded as based in good motives – altruism, cooperation, harmony – with the presumption that these must produce good social results.

However, the link between individual motives and social outcomes is not so straightforward. The Scottish philosopher and economist Adam Smith (1723–90), for

example, showed how self-interest could produce beneficial social outcomes, while the Russian–American writer
Ayn Rand (1905–82) claimed that altruism could only
produce social evil. It is important to look at the motives
that really inspire people under capitalism or socialism,
and trace what good or bad social outcomes they really
produce.

Another common mistake – or deception – of commen-
tators on capitalism is to compare the *reality* of capitalism
with the *ideal* of socialism, often with the excuse that
'ideal socialism has never been tried in practice'. Socialism
can then be portrayed as pure and noble, while capitalism
is blamed for every bad motive, action and result in recent
economic history. But comparing theory to practice is ille-
gitimate: theory must be compared with theory, outcomes
with outcomes. And defenders of capitalism would say it
wins on either test.

There are many other myths and misconceptions. For
example, it is claimed that under capitalism, only a few
individuals own and control capital. Wrong: as the next
chapter will show, we are all owners of capital, to a greater
or lesser extent. Capitalism is also said to be about mass
production using wage labour, which then diverts the discussion into issues of social class and exploitation. Wrong
again: most capitalist enterprises are tiny companies
and sole traders. Capitalism is commonly identified with
profits and markets. Yet these exist in other systems too.
And capitalism is said to mean monopoly and cronyism.
But again, these things are not exclusive to capitalism, but
are promoted by political intervention into it.

The problems of definition

A more realistic definition of capitalism is therefore over-due. We need to clear away the baggage and identify the real concept.

The word *capitalism* itself gives us a clue. The *capital*-part means it is about capital. The *-ism* part means it is about a broad *way of life*. (One could call it a *system* except that 'system' suggests something more centrally designed and managed than capitalism.) At heart, then, capitalism is a way of life that uses capital.

The word *capital* stands for a concept – the abstract idea of the totality of particular *capital goods*. Just as we use the word *animal* to describe an idea that actually exists only in particular hawks, mosquitoes, tigers, spiders, earthworms and dolphins, so the abstract idea of *capital* has reality only in particular capital goods, such as tools, machines and finance. But the idea is not confined to the massive factories, mills and production lines of big businesses. Capital goods are all around us – in every home (washing machines, vacuum cleaners), office (computers, phones), shop (cash registers, display cases), theatre, school and hospital in the developed world.

Why is the use of capital a way of life? Because capital goods enable us to boost the ease and efficiency of producing the things we want. For example, we can produce a lot more bread, with a lot less manual labour, by using farm machinery to plant and harvest the wheat, and electric power to mill the flour and bake the loaves.

Wider associations of capitalism

Economists do not usually include land or labour as capital goods. They see capital goods not as natural resources but as resources that someone creates for the purpose of boosting productivity. Even though capital goods might start as natural materials like trees and iron ore, someone still has to make them into spades and pitchforks.

Capital goods are therefore not like wildernesses or deserts – things that are not owned by anyone. Someone has to invest time and energy in creating them. And it is natural that those who do create capital goods should regard them as their personal property. After all, their effort is an essential part of that capital good, which would not exist without it. The concept of *capital* therefore implies – or at least strongly suggests – the private ownership of capital goods.

This does not mean that capital is owned by only a few rich individuals – the 'wealthy capitalists' of the common caricature. On the contrary, capital goods can be created and owned by anyone, or by groups of people, such as co-operatives or companies. (Some people even talk of 'state capitalism', where governments own and run enterprises – though this seems at odds with the normal use of the word *capitalism*.) Certainly, capitalism works best if capital goods are privately owned and controlled, whether by individuals or close-knit groups. Though private ownership may not be exclusive to (and perhaps not even essential to) capitalism, therefore, it is normally associated very strongly with the concept.

Capitalism is also commonly associated with the distribution of goods through markets. But markets are not the same as capitalism. Capitalism is about the *production* of economic goods; markets are about their *distribution*. Confusing the two leads to serious mistakes about what capitalism is and how it works.

Markets are not exclusive to capitalism: other systems of production use them too. Nor are markets essential to capitalism: the things it produces could be distributed in some other way – by government decree, say, or by lottery. But *some* efficient form of distribution has to be found, if only because capitalism is so very effective at producing things: the huge productivity made possible by the use of specialist capital goods allows people to produce huge surpluses that can then be traded. Markets turn out to be very efficient means of distribution: so again, capitalism and markets generally go together.

Things not essential to capitalism

Many writers, influenced by Marx, suppose that capitalism is necessarily based on a wage system. In their view, capitalist entrepreneurs accumulate capital goods, such as mills and factories, and hire fleets of workers to operate them. This view of capitalism provides these writers with the foundation to contrast entrepreneurs' profit and workers' wages, which they see as the basis of a fundamental class divide, in which workers are exploited by capitalists.

This view is wrong. Capitalism does not necessarily imply a wage system, nor class division. Sole traders, who employ no one, still acquire capital goods: a potter invests in a wheel and a kiln, a shopkeeper in a cash register, a consultant in computers and phones. It is even possible to imagine larger-scale production that is run wholly by machines: indeed, carmakers, online retailers, financial traders and others increasingly use robots to deliver their product. And as a matter of fact, capitalist societies are actually among the most open, socially mobile and least class-bound countries in the world.

Nor is *monopoly* an inevitable part of capitalism. Marx thought that, because of economies of scale, capitalist enterprises would inevitably grow into massive monopolies. But in reality there are *dis*economies of scale too: large enterprises are much more difficult to manage, and much slower to adapt to changes in both technology and consumer demand – giving time for smaller, nimbler competitors to steal business from them. True, producers can and often do try to use political influence to rig markets in their favour: but this is completely contrary to the concept of capitalism, not essential to it. In genuine capitalism, the only way to grow a business is to provide goods and services that people are willing to buy. And with technologies and consumers' tastes changing so fast, that makes it very hard for anyone to maintain a monopoly.

Things not unique to capitalism

There are a number of things that critics think of and write about as being not just essential but unique to capitalism, but which in reality are not. And this is another confusion, or deception, that maligns the reputation of capitalism.

For example, it is often written that capitalism is all about profit: and profit is often assumed to be bad. Both views are mistaken. Profit simply means getting more value out of things than you put in. But profit is not just about money. We pursue non-financial profit in every part of our lives. If we make a hard climb to the top of a hill but are rewarded by a glorious view, or attend a lecture but learn things of great interest, we reckon that we have profited from the effort. And in any economic system, capitalist or otherwise, people hope to obtain similar gains in value. Indeed, economic activity, which involves inputs of time, energy, resources and risk, would be pointless if we valued the goods it produced less than the inputs we spent on producing them.

Nor, oddly, is capital unique to capitalism. Other forms of production also use capital goods. From the hand tools of the most primitive village collective to the mills and factories of the most advanced socialist economy, capital goods are created and used to make production easier and more effective.

Competition – often referred to by capitalism's critics, for polemical effect, as 'cut-throat competition' – is not exclusive to capitalism either. Other systems employ competition for rewards (e.g. financial, political or honorary rewards) as ways of stimulating people into being more hard working, productive, honest or innovative.

Cronyism is not a part of the core concept of capitalism, and is certainly not exclusive to it. The principles of capitalism do not imply an unholy alliance of capital owners and politicians to exploit others. Indeed, those principles limit state power to the *protection* of individuals against coercion and theft, whether from other individuals or from the state and its cronies. In reality, there is much more opportunity for cronyism in socialist societies, where the state has to be large and powerful in order to run things, and there is therefore more state power to be tapped through corrupting politicians and officials.

Exploitation is in fact no part of capitalism. Capitalism delivers its benefits through voluntary exchange, not through forcing people to buy or produce or consume certain things. People are not forced into wage labour for an employer: they can work for themselves; enterprises are not obliged to produce what the state demands; individuals have a choice over what they do and do not buy. And since exchange in capitalism is voluntary, it occurs only where both sides benefit. Like children swapping football stickers, a voluntary exchange leaves each side with something they value more than what they give up: unless both see benefit in the exchange, the trade would never be done at all. It is the same in capitalism: to prosper, producers have to create goods and services that customers value more than the money they tender for them; to find employment worthwhile, workers must value their earnings more than the time and effort they give up. Such voluntary exchanges do not exploit people, but make them better off.

Lastly, *greed* is not exclusive to capitalism; it exists in all economic systems and all walks of life. Capitalism is certainly based on self-interest, which is a natural human characteristic: if we had no regard for our own interests, we would not survive very long. But capitalism punishes greed. Free people simply do not deal with producers they believe dishonest, untrustworthy or focused too much on themselves and too little on their customers. In a competitive economy, there are many other suppliers they can go to. That is why we do not need 'anti-greed' laws to stop cafes overcharging: if they did, their customers would soon desert them. In fact, capitalism is cooperative: we all benefit from collaboration through honest trade; and we all want to live in a world where people deal fairly.

Defining capitalism

How then to define capitalism? At heart, it is a general way of economic life in which people create and apply capital goods in order to produce, as productively as possible, the goods and services that they and others want.

Beyond this core definition, capitalism is also associated with other things that may not be unique or essential to it. For example, it is associated with the ownership of property by private individuals and groups. Property rights – the rules on how property can be acquired, protected, used or given away – are important to capitalism because they enable individuals to create and employ productive goods with confidence.

Capitalism is also associated with market exchange. Other ways of distributing economic goods are possible, but market exchange provides an efficient way of distributing the bounty that capitalism's (also highly efficient) producers can create. In addition, market prices alert producers to customers' preferences – helping them to focus their capital on serving those preferences as efficiently as possible.

Capitalism is usually seen as an economic way of life – about the creation and distribution of economic goods, not about moral or social outcomes. Yet it is in fact a social system – about human interaction on many levels.

It is a highly moral system too. The human relationships in capitalism are not forced but voluntary. People invest, create, supply, sell and buy things as they choose. No government ordains their actions: the decisions are theirs. Indeed, the only role for the power wielded by the state is to ensure that individuals are *not* forced – or robbed, defrauded, or otherwise violated. Capitalism is not based on commands, but on the *rule of law* in which general rules (such as honest dealing, honouring contracts and shunning violence) apply to everyone – including the government authorities.

Yet, like a game that also proceeds by following rules, capitalism does not guarantee any specific result. It cannot be blamed for the crimes, follies or misfortunes of humankind. It does not promise enlightenment or equality. It does not even promise to enrich everyone (though in fact it does). But what capitalism does promise is to boost economic productivity – and boost it in ways that keep opportunities open to all, treat people equally and fairly, and reject fraud, coercion and violence.

3   WHAT CAPITAL IS

The concept of capital

Capital, as we have seen, is an abstract idea, like the concept of *animal*. But while most people can recognise something as an animal when they see it, few people really understand what capital is – even those who own it and use it.

Again, many people picture capital in terms of huge factories, buildings, cranes, metal presses and financial funds, which bolsters the idea that capital is owned only by a wealthy few. But the reality is that capital goods are owned and used by just about everyone in developed countries, and benefit yet others. One might even say that capital goods are democratic.

The purpose of capital

It is worth asking why capital exists in the first place. The answer is that we create capital goods to help us produce, more efficiently, the many goods and services that we need and want. They allow us to produce clothes, food, shelter, lighting, heating, medicine, education, toys, transport, communications, art, entertainment and everything else we want, more cheaply and more efficiently than we could without them.

It is important to remember that the only reason we produce things is because we want to enjoy things. As the Scottish economist Adam Smith (1723–90) put it, 'Consumption is the sole end and purpose of all production.' Yet many critics of capitalism focus on how production should be restructured, without thinking much about *why* we produce things in the first place, or about *what* we want to produce. But our time, effort and mental energy are all far too precious to waste. We need to focus on producing things that we need or want, and on producing them as quickly, easily and cheaply as we can.

How capital boosts productivity

We create and use capital because it makes us more productive. Using boats and lines and nets, for example, we can catch far more fish than we ever could using our bare hands. Using tractors and harvesters, we can farm the land and produce more food with much less effort. Using power looms, we can process more cotton into more clothes more quickly and more cheaply. Using trucks, we can rapidly and easily distribute these products to where they are most needed.

In fact, capital goods can provide quite staggering improvements in productivity, enabling us to produce things in far greater quantity or quality, and at far lower cost. The British author Matt Ridley (1958–) calculates that today's electric lights provide illumination 43,200 times more cheaply than the candles of 1800, while farm production is 600 times higher than in 1900. When books had to be written out by scribes, only the rich few could afford them; printing presses now produce them by the million, with more downloaded online. Cotton clothing was once a luxury too; but the power looms of the Industrial Revolution made it a hundred times cheaper, and available to people across the world. The wristwatches that come off today's production lines are slimmer, more accurate and a thousandth of the cost of the handmade pocket watches in the nineteenth century.

Capital goods even enable us to create things that would be impossible without them. Europeans and Americans today enjoy fresh – no longer pickled – mangos, thanks to refrigerated transport, and air cargo has made them commonplace. Using our smartphones, we can do business with people on the other side of the world, talk to friends on the move, or pull down a vast library of news, information and entertainment – the world's symphony orchestras in your pocket. Nanotechnology allows us to produce solar cells too small to see, films that use light energy to kill germs and fabric that stretches to fifteen times its original size.

As well giving us new, cheaper, better and more plentiful goods and services to consume directly, capital goods also improve the inputs that we make and use in the process of creating these things. For example, machines enable us to mine the iron ore and roll the steel that we use to make cars or washing machines, or to produce the glass we use to make storage jars for our food, or to create the chlorine we use to make the polyurethane that in turn we use to make shoes, beds, window frames and canoes.

Traditional notions of capital

Physical goods. Most people think of capital goods as physical goods like tools, industrial machines, ships, factories, or possibly offices, computers and delivery trucks. Such goods clearly raise our productivity by enabling us to make and deliver things faster, more easily and in greater quantity than we could without them. This much is straightforward.

However, it is often overlooked that capital goods *markets* raise the productivity of these (and other) capital goods still further. New and second-hand markets steer machines, ships, vehicles, equipment and even buildings towards their highest-value uses.

Suppose, for example, that improvements in battery technology mean that many producers start buying more electric trucks and fewer diesel ones to use in their delivery fleets, because they are cheaper, more reliable, quieter and cleaner. That change sends a market signal to truck makers that they must re-tool – adjusting their production lines to meet the new demand and incorporate electric motors instead of diesel ones. In turn, *their* suppliers will find that they are selling fewer diesel engines, and will switch their production lines to making better-selling products. Old diesel trucks and engines, meanwhile, will be scrapped so that the metal can be put to more productive uses, or will be sold cheaply on second-hand markets to customers who still have use for them. In such ways, old and new capital goods are automatically steered to their most productive uses.

Financial capital. Another familiar form of capital is financial capital. Fund managers, for example, borrow money that the banks collect from savers, and use it to invest in businesses that need money to start up or expand. To those businesses, finance is a capital good like any other, enabling them to buy the equipment that they need to produce things efficiently or expand their output to meet the demands of their customers.

The businesses that prove most successful in meeting demand will generate more income from happy customers than those that are less successful: so they can offer investors a better return, and attract more financial capital to their enterprises. As with physical capital, therefore, the financial capital market quickly steers financial capital to its most productive uses.

People often assume that that financial capital, more than any other kind of capital, must be owned by a wealthy few. This is mistaken: the ultimate investors in the funds that in turn invest in businesses are mostly ordinary individuals, saving money for a 'rainy day' or to provide income in their retirement. These are the real 'capitalists'.

Infrastructure. Infrastructure, such as roads, bridges and harbours, are goods that enhance productivity by making commerce easier and cheaper – though they are an odd form of capital, being generally owned by governments rather than private individuals and groups. This allows critics of capitalism to argue that supposedly 'capitalist' enterprises are in fact heavily dependent on the state. But this is to forget that many roads, rail networks and harbours were originally created by private investors, or by the private action of interested citizens – the rest being paid for out of the taxes paid by private individuals and businesses. So even 'public' infrastructure is built on private wealth.

The most important form of capital

Important as they seem, none of these forms of capital is as important as the one that is held by each of us – our *human capital*.

The American economist Gary Becker (1930–2014) did not coin the phrase 'human capital', but worked extensively on the idea. Human capital is all the knowledge and personal qualities that make individuals more productive. It includes our education and skills, but also such qualities as diligence, and even good health. And we invest in these things to make ourselves even more productive, just as we invest in other capital goods.

Thus, we attend schools, colleges and training courses to learn the social and practical skills we need to be productive. What might matter most to us is our earning potential, but if we are more productive, we can generally earn more. Employers invest time and money to train new employees how to operate their machines and information systems. Families teach their children self-discipline, honesty, reliability, punctuality and other values that similarly improve their prospects in work and business. And by investing in our health and fitness, we can remain more productive for longer.

Once again, there are markets to help us maximise our productive potential. They include colleges at which we can earn qualifications, courses on which we can develop our skills, employment agencies that match our skills and personal qualities to the jobs for which we are best suited, fitness clubs that help us stay healthy, and clinics and rehab centres to restore our mental and physical health.

Economists traditionally see labour, along with land, as something different from capital, but the idea of human capital makes this division seem too strict. Human capital makes labour more productive, just as tools and equipment do. Indeed, it is probably more important to productivity than all the other forms of capital put together. Even though capital in general is more widely owned than people imagine, the fact is that *everyone* owns human capital, and most individuals and families invest heavily in it. The successes of immigrants who build successful businesses from nothing – Astor, Carnegie or the founders of Procter & Gamble, Kraft and DuPont – testify to the importance of education, skills and personal qualities such as focus and diligence. As does the wealth of Hong Kong, Macao or Singapore – small places with few natural resources apart from the values and work ethic of their populations.

Even so, human capital needs the right conditions to flourish. It needs people to be free to invest in themselves and their families, and that their right to enjoy the fruits of that investment is respected.

Systems infrastructure

How capital goods are used is an important part of their benefit. The employees of the pioneering car maker Henry Ford (1863–1947) used much the same hammers, spanners or hoists as any other; but he organised this capital on an assembly line that made car making far more productive than any before it. The right *system* is an important capital asset.

Networks. Phone networks, supply chains and distribution systems are other forms of this 'organisational' capital, boosting the efficiency of communications and distribution. Information networks, such as the internet, interactive TV and email raise our productivity too: as well as facilitating production and exchange, they promote the spread of ideas, encouraging innovation and the discovery of new, better productive techniques. They also make possible more efficient ways of working – like 'sharing economy' apps that match families to babysitters, travellers to drivers, and homeowners to those looking for places to stay.

Markets. The market system is not the same as capitalism. But individual markets – whether in goods, services, finance or labour – are arguably a form of capital. They are not just a means of distributing goods and services, but a productive arrangement in their own right.

Like other forms of capital, markets require investment – to develop and police the rules needed to keep them operating, and to maintain the communications and other systems on which buyers, sellers and brokers depend.

They also boost productivity by spreading information about surpluses and shortages. If a popular TV show makes many more people want to visit the place where it was filmed, for example, tour operators find that they can charge higher prices to take people there. They will schedule more flights, trains or buses to that location, taking them off less profitable destinations. In addition, the rise in visitor numbers will allow local restaurants and coffee shops to raise prices, prompting new ones to set up; while local people will find they can earn more as waiters than in other types of work. Through price signals like these, production and capital are steered efficiently and automatically to their highest-value uses.

In fact, market prices coordinate the activities of countless individuals all around the planet. Even in 1776, Adam Smith talked of the vast number of people involved in the production of even a simple woollen coat: shepherds, spinners, weavers, dyers, merchants, sailors, shipwrights, toolmakers, and many more. But none of these individuals intends to produce a particular coat for a particular customer: they merely respond to market prices, which signal where their effort is best applied. And if customer demand (or, for that matter, production technology) changes, prices will change and new signals will ripple through the whole network, prompting everyone concerned to adapt to the new reality.

Through such dynamic coordination, markets boost the productivity of every producer, and every capital good they touch. They reward high-value producers and thoughtful planners, and prompt less effective producers to switch their efforts elsewhere. In so doing, they also conserve resources – after all, nobody wants to waste their time, effort or capital if it could be better used elsewhere.

Legal and cultural capital

Justice. Capitalism is based on voluntary actions and interactions. But such an arrangement can work only if people can act and interact freely, and make plans and investments with confidence. Capitalism therefore requires a system of justice that ensures that people are not subjected to violence, theft or fraud, that contractual promises are honoured, and that individuals' rights and freedoms are respected.

Like markets, the justice system also has the hallmarks of a capital asset. We invest heavily in it (lawmaking, police, courts, prisons, etc.), it is relatively durable, and it makes us more productive by promoting trust and so ensuring that capitalism works smoothly.

There are many parts to this asset. The common law, for example, whereby disputes are settled in court and the acceptable norms of commercial behaviour are established; the *rule of law* under which justice follows due processes, and those in authority are bound by law like the rest of us; and the rules around democracy and representation, with constitutional restraints on the use of government power. All these things promote trust, certainty and security, and so facilitate forward planning, investment and easy dealing in the marketplace, making justice a capital asset that boosts our productivity.

Property rights. People are more likely to make investments and create capital goods if they know they can own and control them, and will benefit from what they produce. So the legal rules and social conventions around the ownership and use of property – what we call property rights – must be relatively certain and durable. But they are not always obvious (e.g. are planes allowed to fly over your property: if so, at what height?). And they do change as circumstances and opinions change (e.g. are you permitted to own and sell cannabis?). Yet by being relatively intuitive and durable, they promote trust and productivity.

Intellectual property – trademarks, copyright and patents – are a special kind of property, being limited in term. The idea behind them is to ensure that inventors, authors and others who build up a valuable brand can enjoy the fruits of those efforts – which benefits us all because it will encourage other innovators to do the same. But there cannot be permission for that business, or that person's heirs and successors, to enjoy a monopoly over the product or invention forever: we want ideas to develop and spread. So we time-limit these protections. The exact rules may vary across the world, but the fact that the general principle is respected still promotes trust and productivity.

Culture and the moral tradition. Capitalism, and the productivity it achieves, benefits from a culture in which there is mutual respect, broadly shared values, trust and a general rejection of the use of force against others. Economic experiments indicate that capitalism and this culture are mutually reinforcing: people from places where markets are well established tend to trust each other more than people from places where markets are less important; and a culture of trust naturally makes commerce easier.

In small, homogeneous societies, trust may come naturally. But in most places, with diverse populations, it has to be built up over centuries. It requires an investment in developing the values and institutions that enable capitalism to work. Since such a culture is something we have to work to create, is relatively durable, and boosts our productivity, it looks very much like a form of capital in its own right.

Conclusion

Exactly how to define capital may be controversial. But it is clear that capital is not confined to an array of factories, heavy machines, ships and financial assets owned by the few. It is much more democratic. We all use capital goods in our homes, shops and offices. We save in banks and financial funds that in turn invest in productive enterprises. We are made more productive by the use of private networks, and public ones built with privately produced wealth.

We use markets and other systems that make their own contribution to our productivity, and strive to maintain a culture of trust. Most of all, we all have human capital within ourselves: our knowledge, skills and abilities. We are all capitalists, and capital is something very diverse – and very democratic.

4   HOW CAPITAL IS CREATED

To understand capitalism, it is important to understand the life of capital: that it does not simply exist, but must be created, is easily lost or destroyed, and requires effort to maintain. Misconceptions about these things lead to a great many misplaced criticisms of capitalism itself.

Mistaken ideas about capital acquisition

Many critics seem to suggest that capital can only be acquired by stealing it from the hard work of others. They argue that employers acquire capital by tricking workers out of the value they create. Or they claim that nations build up their capital by going to war and taking the product of those they conquer. Or they see corporations as using political cronyism to create monopolies that cheat consumers. Capitalists, in other words, become so through deceit, warfare or extortion. And the assumption is that the capital they acquire through these crimes remains with them, providing them continuing benefits with no effort.

These ideas are wrong – or at least, out of date. There was certainly a time when capital was routinely acquired by force: when countries would invade others to take their wealth and then live off the labour of the vanquished; when aristocrats could exploit their serfs; and when monarchs would grant lucrative monopolies to their friends. But that was an age before capitalism, when people were much poorer than today, and could rarely afford to acquire capital goods of their own. In developed countries today, force is outlawed and capital has to be built up through peaceful means, without coercing others. Capital is no longer a rare possession, to be fought over or stolen: it is now much more affordable, and much more widely held, by a much wealthier world population. The only legitimate way to acquire capital today is not to take it from others, but to create it for yourself.

The idea that capital is a permanent asset, which provides its lucky owners with a continuing stream of effortless benefits – like apples falling off a tree – is also mistaken. In fact, capital takes time, money and effort to preserve. It must be maintained and protected. And to keep its value in a changing and competitive world, it must be applied with constant diligence and focus. Even fruit trees have to be cultivated, grafted, watered, sprayed, nurtured and eventually replaced if an orchard is to keep paying its way. Even then the fruit has to be harvested and put to use – distributed to shops, for example, or processed into drinks. If none of this work happens, it will cease to be a valuable orchard and become merely a useless, neglected wilderness: no longer capital, but dross.

Again, it seems, the critics do not see how individualist and democratic capital (and capitalism) actually is. Capital does not simply exist, but must be created. Today it is created and owned by the many, not the few. Its value depends on exactly what those people create and how they protect, maintain and apply it.

Capital is not easy to keep

Capital can also be lost – all to easily – through risk and bad judgement, by consuming it, or through violence and taxation.

Risk and uncertainty. None of us can predict the future with certainty. Nobody can plan for some unexpected event that disrupts our endeavours. Even if we are fairly confident about what the future holds, and calculate the chances of success or failure with care, there is still the risk that we are proved wrong.

So when we invest time, effort or money to create capital goods, we are taking a risk. Our assessment of the future outcomes might be wrong: our investment might produce lower returns than we expect, or even a loss. For example, you might open a pizza restaurant, with all the latest pizza-making technology, only to find that customers prefer a rival's pizzas or have been won over by a health fad and are eating salads instead. If things get really bad, you may have to write off your investment, scrap the capital equipment and close up.

If people think the risks of an enterprise are high, they will invest in it only if they expect the rewards to be high too. But over a long time, even modest risk can destroy people's capital holdings. That is one reason why wealth does not stay permanently in the same hands. Take any magazine from fifty years ago and look at the advertisements: few if any of the companies you see will be familiar to you. Most have long since been driven out of business by competitors with newer, better or cheaper offerings. Family businesses too come and go, as the old adage 'shirtsleeves to shirtsleeves in three generations' proclaims: one person establishes a business, the children inherit and run it, and the grandchildren, born with more money than business sense, ruin it.

Consumption. Profligacy destroys capital – one can consume capital as well as losing it through risk. For example, the owners of a family business might borrow against its security, or sell off its assets, not to invest in new capital equipment but simply to pay their own generous wages. Or the founders might set up a trust fund to support their children and grandchildren – who then (in 'trustafarian' fashion) simply live off that capital instead of putting it to work for the future. Either way, the family consumes its capital. Before long, they are back to shirtsleeves again.

Violence. Capital can of course be lost through theft or fraud, or destroyed through violence. As well as being immoral and causing loss to the victim, such actions impose costs on everyone. Resources have to be spent on investigating and punishing the crime. Even if the crime goes unpunished, the person who takes capital by force will probably extract less value from it than the person who carefully created, focused, managed and applied it to its most productive purpose – creating a loss to the whole community.

The ultimate form of violence is war: and as we have seen, some of capitalism's critics think that war allows the strong to steal capital from the weak. Others claim that business people like (and foment) wars simply because they profit from supplying all the ships, aircraft, electronics, vehicles and weapons that will be needed. But in fact, businesses cannot start wars. Only governments have the power to issue ultimatums or conscript soldiers. And people in business know that wars are not helpful, but highly damaging to them: wars increase risks (which raises the cost of doing business), damage customer confidence and demand, and destroy capital – including physical goods, systems and human capital. This obvious truism is why so few democracies now go to war with others that they trade with. In past centuries, warfare might have been regarded as a good way to grab another country's capital; today we realise that it is easier, safer and more effective not to grab capital from others, but to create it.

Taxation. Capital can be destroyed by less radical forms of state action, such as the taxation of wealth or income.

For example, suppose that in the name of helping the poor and making 'the rich' contribute more to public services, the government imposes a 10 per cent tax on all forms of capital. People who are thinking of creating or expanding a business will now find that the capital goods they need to run it – premises, machines, equipment, vehicles and finance – are now 10 per cent more expensive. That will make them less likely to go ahead with their venture. They will need to be more certain than before that their business will succeed before they risk their money and effort on the enterprise. They will also be less likely to build, expand or replace their capital goods. As a result, productive capacity will be lost, and the whole of the community will be made slightly worse off.

The same is true when wealth in general is taxed. People can leave their money to lie around unproductively, or spend it on today's pleasures. But if they are to turn their wealth into a productive capital asset, they need to apply it to that end with direction and focus. We can encourage that by allowing people to take the full reward of this effort. But when wealth is taxed, that potential reward is lowered and the risk of loss is increased. As a result, people's wealth is used less productively and their financial funds are broken up, dissipated and consumed rather than being used to boost productivity. And that damages everyone.

Redistribution. Redistribution is another policy that destroys capital. Capital cannot simply be taken and given to others without any loss or disruption to its productivity. The productivity of capital depends on many things, such as what it is, where it is, how it is managed and – importantly – how it integrates with other capital. For example, a complex product delivery network is inevitably disrupted if some of its trucks are requisitioned for use by others.

One can see this in countries where farms have been taken from their owners and the land and equipment redistributed to other people. Integrated systems and capital structures are broken up, and too often the result is crop failures and food shortages. Likewise, China's experiment with collective agriculture was a disastrous failure, redeemed only when the country introduced a new 'family responsibility' system that was more akin to private ownership.

Antitrust legislation. Laws aimed at curbing the monopoly power of large companies can also have a damaging effect on the capital network. In an open and competitive economy, companies can grow only by giving customers what they value – not through coercion or cronyism. Their growth is an indication of their success in that. Limits on market share mean that companies that are efficient in using their capital to deliver most value to the public are not allowed to do so, and that capital is drawn instead to less efficient producers.

But there is damage even before that limit is reached. It is very hard to define when a particular firm has become 'dominant' in a market, and whether its large size is more of a threat to customers than an indication of the value that it is delivering to them. The decisions of antitrust legislators are therefore difficult for firms to predict. So they decide to stay small, and the potential gains of their efficiency are lost; or they grow but are then broken up by regulators, causing disruption to their capital network and a resultant loss to customers.

As we have seen, even the largest firms can be threatened by other large companies, or combinations of others, or even by smaller firms chipping away at different parts of their business. So many supporters of capitalism would argue that policy should focus on making markets more open rather than imposing arbitrary size limits on popular and successful producers.

Capital depends on human valuation

Another aspect of the democratic or individualist nature of capital, often lost on the critics, is that capital does not exist on its own, independent of human beings. To be a capital good, and not just a valueless thing, an object must be made to serve human needs, wants and values. A stone is only a stone, of no value until a human realises its productive potential – in building a house, say, or grinding corn. Only then does it become capital. Uranium was thought to be a largely useless (and therefore worthless) mineral, until we discovered how to generate nuclear power. Now a uranium mine is a valuable capital asset.

But if human beings are to transform something from a useless object into a potentially productive capital asset, they need property rights over it. They need to have confidence that they can possess it, manage it, and benefit from its use. Some years ago the Peruvian economist Hernando De Soto (1941–) pointed out that, while many of Peru's poorest people built themselves homes and farmed patches of land, these could not be considered capital because their users had no legal title to them. He campaigned for that to change: and now those same farmers have legal title and are able to use their homes as collateral for loans to buy land and equipment. Their property rights make once-worthless land secure and valuable, prompting them to invest in making it more productive.

Such ideas as property titles, the legal status of ownership, the law making corporations possible, and the regulations and culture of markets are so familiar to people in highly developed Western countries that they are hardly noticed. Nor are they seen, and understood, in countries where freedom is so suppressed and economic power so centralised that no property rights exist. But such rights are legal and cultural assets that are vital to using resources productively.

The real origin of capital

Creating property rights and legal systems is therefore an important way of turning things into capital, and maintaining those systems is critical to capitalism. But beyond that, things are turned into capital only by investing time and effort.

For example, you may be able to catch a few fish with your bare hands; but you will catch far more fish if you fashion a stick into a harpoon, or collect fibres and turn them into fishing nets, or make a boat so you can fish in richer waters.

Where does the considerable time and effort required to create even these simple capital goods come from? The answer is that it has to come out of *consumption*. Instead of instantly consuming every fish you catch, you need to consume less (or spend time catching more) so that you can stockpile enough to live on while you are working to create these new productivity-enhancing tools. That means forgoing consumption – eating fewer fish, or enjoying less leisure time.

Forgoing consumption is the main way that capital is created. You could of course borrow fish from someone else so that you could live at the same standard while making your fishing tools; but eventually you will have to pay that loan back with interest, so even then you will be giving up some of your own consumption, in the future. And (apart from establishing property rights, justice systems, markets and suchlike – all of which require a comparable investment of time and effort) forgoing consumption is the only sustainable way of creating capital.

Capital versus coercion

The lesson is that you have to *save* to *invest* and prosper. But people save only if they have the protection of property rights and the rule of law, giving them the confidence that the capital they create, and the goods it produces, will not be stolen by someone else – including the government – by force or fraud.

In capitalism, the security of property rights and the rule of law promotes the creation of capital, and therefore the higher productivity achievable through specialisation, and the value-creation that comes from the voluntary exchange of the products that this greater efficiency produces. The creation of capital, and indeed capitalism, creates value – at nobody's expense and without coercion.

Government policy is just as critical to capital formation and growth as is the absence of fraud and force by others. Taxes on saving, investment and income give people less incentive to save, invest or create value. Redistribution takes capital from the investors who create, nurture and focus it, putting it into the hands of those (like government officials) who have less interest in doing so, or dissipating it entirely to spend on current consumption. But more than that, such policies break up the delicate network of investments, by which capital goods work together to deliver the most productivity – the *capital structure*.

5   WHY THE CAPITAL STRUCTURE IS CRUCIAL

Mainstream economists often treat capital as homogeneous – uniform, like sand, each portion of which is pretty much like any other bit. In their calculations, models and forecasts, the only concern about it is how much capital there is.

But in reality, capital is very diverse. It exists only in specific capital goods, all of which are different: from hammers and sickles to cars and trucks, cotton mills and car plants, computers and printers, cash registers and freezer cabinets, loans and bonds, and many more. Exactly what kind of capital goods are used, how they are used, and how they network with other capital goods, all have profound effects on economic outcomes.

Failing to understand this leads to serious mistakes. For example, it is nonsense to talk about 'the' return on capital, as the French economist Thomas Piketty (1971–) does in his 2013 book *Capital in the Twenty-First Century*. The different capital goods that comprise capital each come with different amounts of risk and potential reward, and have different owners who have different levels of skill in managing them, and who apply them to different purposes. There are also numerous different ways in which different kinds of capital can be lost, stolen, dissipated, consumed, taxed or regulated away – some more easily than others – all of which eat into the potential return of the various capital goods in various ways and to various degrees. Not only that, but the mix of capital goods that are in use is constantly changing: today we use cars and computers where once we used horse buggies and slide rules. So there is no permanent, uniform profile of a nation's capital with a permanent, uniform 'rate of return'.

The network of productive goods

How the different capital goods are networked with each other is even more important than how many there are or how much has been spent on creating them. Supply chains can be very long, with large numbers of producers in different countries creating the various inputs that feed into to the creation of components and then the final goods and services that we consume.

Take Adam Smith's simple woollen coat again. Not just many people, but a vast array of capital goods must be teamed up to supply this end product. They include the shops and shop fittings of the retailer, the warehouses and trucks of the wholesaler, the looms and sewing machines of the manufacturer, the dye mills and spinning frames of the thread makers, the shears and balers of the shepherds, the smelting works and foundries of those who make the tools and equipment used by all of these people, the ships and planes of the hauliers who move the raw materials and equipment used at each stage – plus the many others that all contribute to supplying this simple, everyday item. Even then, the process would not be viable without the diverse capital equipment needed to supply the many people who work in this process with the food, drink and housing they need, and indeed their own clothes too.

Plainly, the absence of any one of these capital goods could disrupt the entire manufacturing process, creating shortages, supply problems and logistical nightmares for every operation further along the chain. Without the dye mill, for example, the finished wool cannot be supplied to the weavers and finishers, and thence the garment cannot be sent to the wholesaler, the retailer and the customer.

How the vast, global array of capital goods is networked together, therefore, is absolutely crucial to maintaining and improving the productivity and efficiency with which goods are created. That includes both the goods used in production and the goods that go to customers – the consumption goods like the woollen coat, which are the whole purpose of all this effort.

Our productivity therefore depends on not just the amount of capital or the number of factories, machines, trucks and tools we have. The capital structure, how our capital goods are networked together, is critical to how we create the goods and services we need and want, and how efficiently and productively we create them.

The fragility of the capital structure

The critical importance of this capital structure is often overlooked by political visionaries or economic planners who think that capital can be taken from its owners, redistributed to others, or put to 'more rational' uses, without any loss to the value it produces – and indeed, often in the expectation that, in these new hands, capital will become more productive and produce things of higher value than it does now. But the simple truth is that there would at the very least be a massive disruption to production.

Economic planners should remember that this elaborate structure of capital goods, spanning many countries, many product sectors and many processes, is the result of an evolutionary process by which each part of the network is constantly adapted and reshaped by capital owners in order to meet the changing requirements of customers and to produce the things that people value most highly. For example, if the weather gets warmer and shoppers start demanding cotton clothes instead of woollen ones, retailers and wholesalers start ordering more cotton goods, manufacturers retool to produce them, suppliers start buying more cotton and shippers switch their routes to bring more raw cotton from the plantations, where farmers will be growing more cotton to meet the new demand. Like ripples spreading out when a stone is thrown into a pond, the whole process adapts to the new reality, reassigning or replacing the individual parts of the capital structure as needed.

Planners should also remember that capital is not homogeneous, and not all capital goods can be reassigned to other uses when circumstances change. Some, such as a pair of scissors, a sewing machine or a truck, can be used for many different purposes: they will cut, stitch or transport cotton cloth just as well as they do woollen cloth. But the industrial-scale looms that weave the cloth may require extensive adaptation to handle the new, finer cotton thread. At worst, they and other machines used in the manufacture may have to be scrapped completely, and new purpose-made machines brought in.

The fact that some capital goods cannot be adapted to another purpose is another reason why capital ownership does not guarantee owners a secure and comfortable return. When circumstances change, some capital goods may have to be written off – leaving owners with a real loss. The domestic spinning wheels and handlooms of Scottish wool weavers, for example, became of scant value once water-powered spinning frames and looms were invented. And many of those machines themselves had to be adapted to process the new cotton fibre coming from the New World. Today, those machines and the mills that housed them are largely dismantled and demolished – or turned into offices, exhibition spaces or museums – because the UK now imports so much of its clothing from India, China, Nepal and other developing markets.

Not even state industries are immune from capital losses. The Zwickau factory in East Germany, which had made Trabant cars since 1957, lost its entire purpose once Germany was reunified and people could buy faster, quieter, cleaner and more comfortable alternatives, and was left an empty, rotting hulk. As, indeed, was a great deal of the outdated and useless capital of the former Soviet Union.

Bad policy kills capital

Capital can be lost, then, just because it is no longer the right stuff in the right place at the right time. As technology develops, and as customers' needs, wants and tastes change, the capital structure has to adapt to reflect those changes – and some capital may simply not be adaptable and will have to be written off. But as we have seen, there are lots of other ways by which capital can be lost, including the mistaken forecasts, bad judgement or poor management of its owners.

Public policy can also disrupt the capital structure and destroy capital – and not always intentionally. One example is the boom–bust trade cycles (also called business cycles) that many countries experience. Booms might happen because new technology makes lots of things better or cheaper – as did the invention of the steam engine, electricity or the internet. But that does not lead to a bust, unless people grossly overestimate the potential benefits of the new technology and over-invest on that basis.

What then causes the boom–bust cycles that are so common and so frequent? The Austrian economists F. A. Hayek (1899–1992) and Ludwig von Mises (1881–1973), who studied these cycles, concluded that they were typically set off by bad public policy. They start with governments trying to stimulate economic activity and boost employment by keeping interest rates down or adding to the amount of money in circulation. With more money in their pockets, customers spend more, and spend proportionately more on expensive and sophisticated products, which they can now afford. With borrowing cheap because of the low interest rates, producers seek to capture some of that demand by investing in new plant and equipment to produce all these goods.

But just as the high delivered by alcohol or amphetamines is followed by the pain of a hangover, so is this money and credit boom followed by a bust. People save less because the returns on their savings are lower. So the banks find they have insufficient funds for all the new borrowing, and start calling in loans. Facing a credit crunch, customers revert to buying cheaper and more basic products. But producers have already built the factories and bought the equipment needed to create the luxuries that people are no longer buying. Those capital goods now have no purpose: production lines are closed down, machines scrapped and workers laid off – and the shops who depended on those workers' spending suffer a downturn, and some will have to close. It was a fake boom built on cheap credit and easy money, but it produces real losses.

Such catastrophes – like the boom and subsequent financial crash in the early 2000s – are not caused by bankers or greed or any of the other popular explanations. They are caused by the state authorities trying to stimulate economic growth, and in the process sending out false signals that disrupt the delicate capital structure network. The damage done by such bad policy is much larger than any caused by the mistakes or ineptness of any individual capital owner, or the replacement of any one technology by another. Boom–bust cycles affect every part of economic life: the losses are not confined to one company or sector, but widespread and systematic. The illusion of prosperity created by the authorities' short-sighted policy is short-lived; yet it leads to real losses, layoffs and bankruptcies – and often failures of the banks themselves – that rip right through the capital structure and the economy as a whole.

Conclusion

Summing up, then, capital is not some homogeneous thing that can be shuffled around at will but without any disruption or cost; nor is it a permanent source of secure income for its supposedly lucky owners. On the contrary, capital exists only in specific capital goods, such as specific tools or machines, or the human capital of individual people's specific skills and knowledge. These capital goods each have different characteristics – being more durable or less, being usable for several purposes or only one, being adaptable to changing needs or not, having at least some scrap value or not, and so on.

Moreover, the productivity that is made possible by these capital goods, and the income boost that follows from that productivity, is not confined to their owners but shared to some extent by the whole population. Everyone in a country benefits from its roads, utility networks, and the literacy and skills of their fellow citizens, and enjoys goods and services that are better and cheaper as a result of producers investing in more efficient processes and equipment.

But these benefits are not permanent. Capital can be lost or stolen; it can decay or be consumed; it can be mismanaged or misapplied; it can be made redundant by new technologies or by the changing tastes of the consuming public. Capital is no magic money tree for a lucky few: it has to be created, nurtured, protected and managed. This is no mean task.

Lastly, capital has to be networked. Today, many production processes are long and complicated, requiring the input of raw materials and parts that come from all over the world, and which in turn rely on other complex international operations to gather, process and assemble them. The capital goods that are used throughout such production need to be operated in concert at every stage.

It is therefore a big mistake to suppose that we could take control of a nation's capital (or the world's) and costlessly redirect it to produce some more valued outcome. It might seem theoretically possible, but it is highly unlikely: after all, many or all of those same capital goods have been created with the specific purpose of being a part of this complex international network of production. It is rather like imagining that we can reorder the pieces of a jigsaw to produce a more pleasing picture: but the pieces do not easily fit together any other way; and the pieces are quite unlikely to produce a better picture. If we are to create a new picture, we need to create and assemble new pieces; likewise, to create different products, we need to create different capital goods and match them together in a coherent productive structure. That is better done by a long, continuing, evolutionary process of trial and error in the marketplace than by the fickle and politically made decisions of some planner, dictator or legislator.

6 WHAT MAKES CAPITALISM WORK

As we have seen, there are a number of things that are not unique to capitalism, or even essential to it, but which are commonly associated with capitalism because they definitely contribute to its success. Among these are self-interest, private property, peace, profit, competition, specialisation and markets.

Self-interest, property, profit and incentives

Self-interest. Capitalism is motivated by self-interest, but punishes greed. The two are quite different.

Greed suggests acting on one's own interests, without a care for the interests or feelings of others, and perhaps even without a care for the prevailing laws, regulations and conventions. It also suggests accumulating things for the sake of it, regardless of one's need. But capitalism can only work when people follow the rules, deal fairly with each other, and honour promises. Fortunately, thanks to the competition from many other buyers and sellers, anyone who lies or cheats in business will soon find customers and suppliers deserting them. The only way to prosper is to provide others with what they want. Far from disregarding the interests of others, capitalism makes us keen to know them and serve them.

Self-interest, by contrast, is a natural human characteristic, without which none of us would survive. The moral question is how to restrain it and steer it into producing a functioning society rather than a chaos of self-serving individuals. Fortunately again, capitalism harnesses self-interest for the benefit of everyone.

Self-interest means people pursuing their own aims, vision, purposes and ambitions, not those imposed on them by others. They pursue those dreams not just for their individual benefit but for the benefit of their families and others whom they love and care about. They collaborate with others, in trade for example, when it is in the mutual interest of both sides. But while the motive might be self-interest, that does not imply some undesirable result. On the contrary, collaboration through trade produces a social outcome that is generally beneficial – as Adam Smith explained with his idea of the 'Invisible Hand'.

Private property. Private property is not unique to capitalism, but is necessary for it to work well. Unexpectedly, perhaps, private property promotes a society that is industrious, mutually respectful, honest and trusting.

It is a fact of life that people take more care of their own property than other people's. In many countries, for instance, the staircases and communal areas in apartment blocks are neglected and decayed, though the apartments themselves are kept beautifully by their owners.

People also extract more value from the things they own privately, to the benefit of both themselves and society. The collective farms of Soviet Russia or Mao's China produced little except widespread starvation, while the privately run farms of capitalist societies are managed carefully to produce the maximum possible yield. The world's oceans, owned by nobody, are over-fished, while Scotland's salmon stocks are fiercely protected by the private owners of the rivers they swim in, whose living depends on them being available for sport.

For people to protect, nurture and extract value from property, they have to be confident in their ownership. There must be clear rules about how property is held, what can be done with it, what benefits can be obtained from it, and how it can be transferred to others. Agreements around the sale or purchase of property – not just land or capital goods but any consumable good or service too – must be clear and respected. Theft and fraud must be rejected, which implies some system of justice and restoration if they occur. Only then can people make future commitments to trade, or to invest in an enterprise that might involve risk and take many years to reach fruition. Capitalism can only work in such a world.

And of course the authorities have to be under the same rule of law as everyone else. They cannot use their political or judicial power to favour some groups or distort markets to achieve some preordained objective; to do that risks throwing markets out of kilter, and destroying the complex network of efficient capitalist production.

Profit. Profit is also not unique to capitalism. In fact we seek it from every activity we engage in, for there are many kinds of profit apart from financial gain. Whatever we do in life, we hope that the benefit that results will be greater than the time and effort we have put in. Was the view worth the climb? Did you learn something really useful from sitting through that long lecture? If so, you have profited.

Even in commerce, profit is not just financial gain. Most people certainly enter business to make money – not necessarily to make a fortune, but to make enough to provide for themselves and their family. Yet nobody wants to do this at the expense of being miserable or continually fatigued. That would be a loss. Among the non-financial profit that different people look for in their economic lives are pride in their work, opportunities for leisure, and the thought that they are doing something useful that helps others. To most of us, perhaps, the contentment we derive from such things is worth more than money.

It is often said that the financial profit made by capitalist entrepreneurs must come out of the wages of workers, through some kind of exploitation. But then entrepreneurs who employ nobody can still make profit, which seems to refute the argument. Second, nobody is forced to work for a particular entrepreneur: so why should they accept work that exploits them? They can easily go to another employer, or work for themselves.

Third, and most importantly, the argument forgets that profit, and value, are created. There is not a fixed pot of value entrepreneurs can get their hands on only if they wheedle employees out of it. Value exists in our minds, not in things: one person might see a particular vase as priceless while the other regards it as junk. And precisely because people value things differently they can trade them and each consider themselves better off. The entrepreneur does not steal value from the employees, but creates it by managing their talents to make something new.

Entrepreneurial profit. An entrepreneur's profit may come from many sources. From trading on differences in people's valuation of things, for example, or from skilfully marshalling inputs, labour, manufacturing processes, marketing and distribution so as to satisfy consumers' demands more effectively. Or it can come from spotting opportunities that others have overlooked.

Some entrepreneurs, for example, profit by spotting a potential demand that others have not seen – as Sony did with its Walkman personal music player, or Starbucks did with their specialist coffee shops. Sometimes, entrepreneurs can profit by inventing new technology, as Eli Whitney did with the cotton gin and Thomas Edison did with the incandescent light bulb. Others profit by applying existing technologies to create new products and processes, as James Dyson did with vacuum cleaners and Apple did with the iPhone.

Entrepreneurs may find ways to enhance customers' convenience, as Amazon did with online shopping, or develop completely new markets and ways of working, as Uber, AirBnB and many other 'sharing economy' apps have done. And regulatory reform can also create new entrepreneurial opportunities. Mobile phone networks, for example, grew rapidly after the breakup of the Bell Telephone Company in the US and the British Telecom monopoly in the UK.

Undoubtedly, a few people have made fortunes from lucky accidents, producing or discovering something that captures the public imagination and becomes a runaway success. And people do occasionally find that the painting they bought in a junk shop is actually an Old Master. But it would be wrong to think that such pure entrepreneurial profit, as it is called, is merely a matter of luck and undeserved. Most entrepreneurs actually work hard for their success and have to put time and effort into promoting their product. They suffer failure and rejection, but carry on until they succeed: twelve publishers rejected J. K. Rowling's first *Harry Potter* novel before Bloomsbury accepted it – with no great expectations of its success.

Incentives. Entrepreneurial profit, therefore, is rarely luck, or even mostly luck: it is an active pursuit that demands the investment of vision, intelligence, time, effort, skill, risk-taking and persistence. Most such efforts will end in failure: but those that succeed improve the lives of everyone, and build the foundations for further progress.

That makes it vital to have a legal, political and social culture that encourages and rewards entrepreneurship and the investment and personal qualities on which it rests. Chief among these is the security of peace and the rule of law, so that entrepreneurs know that they can make such investments with confidence, without their work being destroyed, or their creations stolen, by others – not just by foreign armies and domestic criminals, but also their own governments. Since the risks of failure are already high, for example, entrepreneurs are easily discouraged by high taxes and onerous regulations, which increase their risks and costs even further.

The process of competition

Another thing that makes capitalism so dynamic is competition. To stay ahead of the competition, and stop their customers defecting to others, producers must constantly innovate and improve what they offer and how they produce it.

The economics textbooks rarely explain this dynamic effect of competition. Too often, they talk of 'perfect competition' – a theoretical state in which large numbers of similar buyers and sellers trade identical goods. But in reality, buyers and sellers are all different. And, from trading identical products, sellers are anxious to distinguish them – to offer buyers something unique and more desirable than the competition.

Unfortunately, the 'perfect competition' idea is so widespread that even the defenders of capitalism generally fail to understand how competition really works; while the misleading term 'perfect' makes capitalism's critics (even friendly ones) think that governments must intervene to make markets more 'perfect'.

But real markets never settle in 'perfect' balance: competition is a constant process of adjustment, innovation and improvement, which is the big benefit that competition delivers to us. As entrepreneurs strive to meet our changing needs, new products and processes supplant less effective ones. Customers drive this dynamic process, not officials. Officials' attempts to make markets 'perfect' simply freezes them in some particular state; but under real competition, customers are ruthless at demanding better and better goods from producers, who in turn actively seek out better and better ways to deliver them.

Some businesses may not survive this process. But market competition is not like biological competition, where there is a fixed supply of resources, with life and death hinging on who gets them. Competition creates resources and expands total value. Because businesses face daily testing in the marketplace, they must keep switching resources from lower-value to higher-value uses. Nobody dies: they just have to work differently.

Specialisation and markets

Specialisation and its benefits. Capital goods can be very specialised. Many exist solely to create one particular product or component. In some cases they can make products or components thousands of times more quickly or cheaply. For example, they enable steel to be mined and smelted, engine blocks cast and finished, and cars assembled by the thousand, far faster and cheaper than doing everything by hand. Skills too are specialised: decorators, roofers, glaziers, electricians and plumbers can maintain our homes and services far better and more safely than we could do ourselves, while specialist physicians can know more about our medical ailments than even their non-specialist colleagues.

Ordinary people cannot know everything about every medical condition, or how best to paint a room or fix a washing machine; nor can everyone own the capital equipment needed to make a car. Indeed, it would be very wasteful if we each attempted to. Instead, we all gain from other people's specialisation, in both the skills and the capital goods they acquire. Our cars, watches, haircuts and all the other things we want become cheaper and better thanks to other people's specialisation.

Markets. In fact, specialisation makes capitalism so productive that it becomes urgent to find an equally efficient way of distributing all the goods and services that it creates. This is why markets have developed alongside capitalism. They allow us to trade the huge surpluses we can produce, and to benefit from the fruits of other people's productivity too.

Market exchange occurs because different people value the same goods or services differently. Value is not an objective quality of things like weight or size: value exists only in the mind of the beholder. After swapping something we value less for something we value more, either directly or using money, we consider ourselves better off – as does the person we trade with. Even though our exchange has created no new goods, it has increased total value.

This is particularly important, given capitalism's huge productivity. For example, a cereal farmer, using large-scale mechanised ploughing, seeding and harvesting methods, can personally consume only a tiny portion of the wheat or barley that is produced, and values the crop only for what it can be exchanged for in the market. The same is true of the potter who has little personal use for all the cups and bowls that come off the wheel each day. Likewise for the car maker, the shoemaker, the skilled watercolour artist or the restaurateur. But markets get all their products to customers who value them far more.

Exchange is ancient; but as markets grow and become established, the rates at which different things usually exchange – their prices – become more generally known and predictable. That itself is a benefit to everyone, because it gives us all a better idea of where our investment of resources is most likely to pay off. It also helps producers to get the best price for their goods: the spread of web-enabled phones, for instance, means that small farmers in even the most remote areas of the world can check international food markets and make sure that wholesalers are giving them a reasonable price for their crops. And a look at the futures markets will help them decide what they should plant, and when, to have the best prospect of a good return.

Markets are governed by law and convention, but must adapt to changing customer demand. They need to deal with new products and processes, such as sharing-economy apps. All innovation poses challenges for market regulators: there may be genuine safety concerns about whether new products should be traded, often fuelled by the lobbying of incumbents who fear the competition. But there are benefits too from keeping markets open, particularly when suppliers can be instantly and easily rated online. Only if we allow innovation can we make progress.

Capitalism and the state

Supporters of capitalism argue that the state should neither own nor direct the use of capital goods. They see politicians and public officials as too swayed by narrow political interests rather than the broad needs of consumers. At most, the state should defend the principles that make capitalism work – individual rights, justice and non-coercive cooperation. To do that, it needs its own coercive force – police, armies, courts and prisons. But all power is corrupting and prey to vested interests, so government power should be limited.

Capitalism's supporters argue that individuals can decide most things for themselves, but for collective projects – defence, say, or new airports and roads – democracy is a reasonable way to make decisions. They also see democracy as a peaceful way of restraining and, when necessary, removing those who wield the state's coercive power.

But to work, democracy itself must be limited. It is not a good way of deciding everything, and it brings politics even into those decisions we cannot make in any other way. Nor does democracy mean that a majority of 51 per cent can decide every aspect of the lives of the minority 49 per cent, or exploit them as they choose: democracy requires a culture of toleration and self-restraint. Both citizens and politicians should understand these limits; but too often, they are so proud of democracy's achievements that they think many more things should be decided democratically. Unfortunately, that means deciding more things politically – which opens up tension and conflict and leaves us all exposed to exploitation by the majority.

Constitutions can help keep democracy focused on the functions that it performs well, and protect minorities. To achieve that, they need to be widely supported and relatively permanent, with super-majorities needed to amend them. But no document can guarantee the individual rights and defend the institutions that make capitalism work. Only hearts, minds, morality, culture and tolerance can achieve that.

7   THE MORAL DIMENSION OF CAPITALISM

The socialist and capitalist moral vision

In his 2014 book *Why Not Capitalism?* the American political scientist Jason Brennan (1979–) contrasts the socialist and capitalist moral case.

The socialist idea of the good society, he says, is well known. As on a family camping trip, everyone acts with virtue and public spirit towards an agreed purpose, focusing on the good of everyone, not just themselves. Capitalism can never achieve such harmonious cooperation because it is built on the vices of self-interest and greed. Indeed, the only reason we tolerate capitalism at all is that we are not yet good enough for socialism, lacking the moral strength to completely abandon selfishness and live for the benefit of all.

But an equally compelling case can be made for capitalism, says Brennan. It is built on mutual assistance through reciprocity. It rejects force and exploitation.

It rewards those who benefit others, which fosters trust and collaboration. It allows people to pursue their own purposes freely and peacefully, rather than forcing them to serve some single purpose chosen by those in power. This same diversity promotes toleration for others, respect for their different ambitions and lifestyles, and care for them as individuals rather than mere components in an economic machine. This human care is expressed through the charities, churches and other voluntary institutions of civil society – all given added strength by the wealth that a capitalist society generates.

This vision of capitalism is also more realistic. Capitalist principles can work over the whole world, not just in small groups, while the socialist model of the family camping trip soon breaks down when strangers are added. And there is no point blaming that on our moral weakness. Capitalism does not require us to be saintly altruists, but converts our natural self-interest into social benefits. By rewarding talent, focus, energy and productive organisation, it automatically steers us into innovation, discovery and service to others.

Capitalism creates value and spreads wealth

Capitalism's ability to create and spread value and wealth is another of its moral virtues. Capitalism incentivises people to discover what other people want and provide it. Through the application of highly productive capital equipment, it enables us to satisfy the needs of the many, not just the few.

Not surprisingly, the growth of capitalism has produced a major increase in human incomes and wealth. For most of the long course of human history, average incomes were at subsistence level: perhaps $1–3 a day in modern terms. But around 1800, incomes very suddenly spiked upwards and their skyward rise still continues. The poor have gained particularly: in 1990, according to the World Bank, about 40 per cent of the human population lived on less than $1.90 a day; today it is less than 10 per cent. Poverty has been cut more in the last 35 years than in the last 3,500.

As well as enabling people to afford more of what they need and want, capitalism also enables them to afford better. Competition pushes producers to innovate, to curb prices and raise standards. As a result, all the essentials – food, shelter, fuel and clothing – are now cheaper and higher quality than ever before. In 1800, few people anywhere in the world could afford fresh meat; today, everyone in the capitalist countries can. In 1800, says the British political and natural scientist Matt Ridley (1958–) in his 2011 book *The Rational Optimist*, a candle providing one hour's light cost six hours' labour. By the 1880s, the same light from a kerosene lamp took 15 minutes' work to afford. Now, with LEDs, it is half a second. In lighting terms, we are 43,200 times better off than in 1800.

This huge rise in wealth is why humans today are healthier, taller and longer-lived than ever before. It cannot be explained by some supposedly inevitable march of technology. After all, what spurs technological developments if not the incentives of capitalism? Why did the Great Enrichment occur so suddenly? And why, when West Germans were driving luxurious high-tech Mercedes and BMWs, were East Europeans still struggling to own unreliable, uncomfortable, high-polluting Trabants and Yugos?

Better technology certainly boosts our living standards, but it is capitalism that provides the incentive to develop it. Property rights are essential to that: they give people the means and the confidence to invest time and effort on research, invention and development, knowing that they can reap its rewards. And those new technologies and products are spread widely and speedily through hugely efficient capitalist production and market distribution.

That is why the rapid decline in world poverty since the 1980s is due largely to the opening up of China, India, Eastern Europe and others to international trade and capitalist principles. Singapore, Hong Kong, Taiwan, Japan and South Korea were some of the world's poorest countries at the end of World War II; but just a few decades of trade and capitalism has turned them into some of the world's richest – unlike their near neighbours North Korea, Cambodia and Laos, or even Malaysia and China, which are only recently catching up. Such examples make the point that it is the poorest that have most to gain from capitalism and trade. And for the poorest, an extra $1 a day can mean the difference between life and death.

The human benefits of property rights

Property rights do not just allow people to *use* resources. They give them an incentive to protect, develop and grow resources. Private property is much better looked after, and more productively used, than property owned in common, or owned by nobody. An obvious example is the dismal failure of collective farms in the Soviet Union and in

Mao's China, which produced only famine and destitution. Fisheries are another: being owned by nobody, sea fish stocks are often overfished. Only in places like Iceland and New Zealand, which give fishing fleets tradeable quotas – effectively, a property right in the fish – are stocks well protected.

Property rights also allow people to express and develop themselves as they choose. Property provides a refuge against intrusion by others, or even by the state. As the Anglo–Austrian political scientist and economist F. A. Hayek (1899–1992) pointed out in his 1944 book *The Road to Serfdom*, people cannot even express and discuss different political opinions if a hostile government controls the meeting halls, paper supplies and media.

Property also satisfies something natural within us. The things we own are extensions of ourselves. They may include things that we collected as children, or were given to us by dear friends, or which remind us of places we have been or things that have happened to us. They may be things (such as cars and washing machines) that give us some benefit, convenience and independence. They may be things that we simply enjoy having, maintaining, managing, protecting and developing: many householders would say this of their own homes, for example, and many entrepreneurs would say it of their own businesses.

Some anti-capitalists argue that resources should be shared, not owned. But valued resources do not just *exist*, ready to be shared out as we choose: they have to be created. A barren desert is merely that until some person sees its potential, and clears it for farming, digs an oil well or builds on it. Forcibly sharing out a resource that has taken someone insight and effort to create is not only unjust but counterproductive: for why should anyone go to that effort if they see no gain from it? They might as well idle and wait for a share of other people's effort.

Equality and prosperity

Much has been written about the supposed inequality of wealth and incomes in capitalist societies; and how this justifies redistribution. But the facts do not support the argument. Inequality figures usually look at incomes before taxes and social benefits are taken into account. But after the highest earners have paid taxes and the lowest earners have received welfare, unemployment, sickness or retirement benefits, the resulting income distribution shows little difference between capitalist and socialist countries. The difference is even narrower when one includes state-run services that are provided free to the poorest, as healthcare and schooling often are. Moreover, the statistics generally ignore any dynamic effects. On the logic of one annual survey, the world's poorest people are young Americans who have recently graduated from Ivy League colleges: their large student loans give them 'negative wealth'; but armed with their prestigious qualifications, this same group will end up among the world's wealthiest.

Inequality is a natural consequence of exchange. When thousands of people each pay a few dollars to attend a concert by a popular singer, the singer ends the evening with more dollars, the audience with fewer. The only way to prevent the inequality growing still greater would be to redistribute the singer's earnings after every performance. Financial equality requires continuous redistribution – which leaves people like this singer with no reason to continue performing.

That means that everyone else is denied the non-financial benefits of the transaction. No exchange happens unless both sides gain value: the concertgoers may end the evening a few dollars poorer, but in exchange they have had the exhilaration and enjoyment of listening to someone they admire. That non-financial value cannot be taken from them and redistributed to others. In terms of equalising things of value, the redistribution of financial resources does only half the job.

The problem of defining equality

Under capitalism, financial inequality reflects how well or poorly you serve other people. Financial reward comes only from serving others, and reflects what others are willing to give you for that service. No board or committee is needed to assess the value you provide to others and decide the size of your reward: those you serve judge it for themselves.

Indeed, no board or committee of the state could decide rewards rationally. On what basis would they decide the value to society delivered by a rock star, a sports personality, a deep-sea diver, a teacher, a welder or a nurse? How would they decide how much each should be paid in order to reflect that value? Even if they chose the easy route and paid everyone equally, that would still not achieve either fairness or equality. After all, some jobs are risky, others safe; some enjoyable and varied, some boring and frustrating; some easy, others requiring great concentration; some workplaces are pleasant and convenient, others not. Equal pay does not equalise these differences in psychological income. But under capitalism, competition in the labour market does it automatically: people will demand higher pay, for example, to do jobs that are dangerous or unpleasant or require great skill.

To the supporters of capitalism, therefore, financial redistribution is irrational because there is no objective basis for deciding value and reward; it is skewed because it does not take account of non-financial factors; and it is unnecessary because the market does a better job quickly and automatically. But they also argue that redistribution is immoral. People should have a right to the rewards that come from their talent and hard work. We do not allow individuals to steal money from better-off people, even in the name of equality. So why should we allow the government to do it – particularly since, without any rational basis, the decisions will come down to the whim of officials.

If we genuinely want to help the poor, capitalism seems the best method. In today's global trading economy, it is not the rich but the poor who are getting richer faster: and to the poor, that makes a profound difference. Furthermore, capital makes everyone richer, not just those who happen to own it. By raising productivity, it gives each of us more of what we need and want. It enables us to create more by working less, and in easier conditions. And because the citizens of capitalist countries are richer, they tend to be more philanthropic, sending more of their income to charities. Even without charitable support, however, it is still far better (in terms of income, nearly ten times better) to be poor in a rich capitalist country than poor in a poor socialist one.

Capitalism improves human relations

The American political thinker Ayn Rand (1905–82) argued that capitalism was the only moral social system because it alone did not rely on force to sustain it. Rather, it works only through voluntary exchange. Nobody is forced to deal with anyone else. To persuade people to trade with you requires mutual respect and trust – something of particular value to the poorest.

Capitalism also drives out discrimination. No laws or regulations are needed to achieve this: a business that refused to take on workers of a certain gender, race, religion or culture, or that refused to sell or rent its product to customers from particular groups, would soon find itself undercut by competitors who did not discriminate in this way. Indeed, regulations are often positively harmful for minorities: minimum wage regulations, for example, make hiring people more expensive for employers, so they become less willing to take on and train up untested youngsters or immigrants who may be less fluent in the local language and less familiar with the cultural norms – the very sorts of people that the legislation is intended to help.

Interestingly, capitalism is associated with higher rates of female literacy, which is an important determinant of family health, education and prosperity. Female literacy started to rise rapidly alongside the growth of trade in Renaissance times. Most merchants being men, it would be up to their wives to manage the business while they were at sea or out selling their wares: so female literacy and numeracy became important, as they still are in capitalist societies today.

Comparing like with like

To repeat: one cannot legitimately compare ideal socialism with real capitalism. Nor can one legitimately define socialism in terms of supposedly good motives (such as trust and cooperation) and capitalism in terms of bad ones (such as greed). Many try, but the facts refute them. Capitalism is not cut-throat but cooperative. In fact it is a remarkably cooperative social order that runs on trust and systematically punishes antisocial motives.

Capitalism is also a realistic social system. It focuses our efforts on what actually works – not on some unattainable vision of a perfect society of universally virtuous and altruistic citizens. It has no illusions about human nature. It does not suppose that people can be turned into angels, either by exhortation or force. Instead it works to harness our natural self-interest and channel it to serve a beneficial social outcome. It is also morally consistent: it does not suppose that theft, monopoly, favouritism and force are good just because the state does them.

The capitalist vision can also be expanded beyond the small group. Much of the world is already capitalist, or trades with capitalist countries. Because capitalism works through general rules such as property rights, honesty and respect for contractual agreements, there are no limits on the number of people who can join it. But when societies are directed by some collective goal, large size causes even larger problems. Those who plan and manage them need to collect and process far more information about what should be produced and about how each individual should play their part in that process. There is greater scope for disagreement about what the society's goals should be, and what needs to be done to achieve them. And that puts a premium on leaders who are ruthless enough to make those decisions and purge any disagreement.

8 THE SHORT HISTORY OF CAPITALISM

Twisting capitalism to fit the theory

Karl Marx saw capitalism as merely one stage in an inevitable progression of history. Eventually, he thought, capitalism would be brought down by its internal contradictions and supplanted by communism. This historical analysis is still influential among socialists and social theorists today. As a result, much of the academic and intellectual discussion about capitalism presents it only in terms of its historical development, while the discussion of contemporary capitalism focuses only on the problems that are thought to undermine it.

These preconceptions, therefore, already lead to a misleading view of capitalism that serves the purposes of its critics. Worse, the facts themselves are often distorted to make them fit the theory. Histories are written about economic arrangements that are described as capitalism, but which in reality have scant relation to the actual concept. Moreover, capitalism is blamed for social problems that it never promised to relieve, and for economic problems that owe more to the actions of politicians than of businesses.

It is hard to write a history, or even a description, of something that has never actually existed in its pure form. This point is often raised in order to insulate the pure concept of socialism from criticism of its practical performance – a history marked by dictatorships, purges, genocides, disastrous ecological mistakes, famines, dismally low economic growth and shortages. Supporters of capitalism, however, are less embarrassed by its practical expressions. They admit its problems, but point out that its history is marked by rapidly increasing and spreading wealth, democracy, personal freedom and peace. So even if pure capitalism has never existed, it is still instructive to explore the history of those societies that have adopted at least some version of its principles.

State-directed commerce

The period from the sixteenth to the nineteenth centuries was characterised by economic nationalism and the desire of monarchs and ministers to build economically strong states. They saw this as requiring their countries to sell as much as they could to others, and to buy as little from others as they could, in order to boost their own earnings and accumulate as much wealth – in gold and silver – as possible. They believed that only sellers benefited from an exchange, since it is sellers who end up with the money. The gold and silver that poured into a nation's vaults was the source and measure of its prosperity and power.

Trade policy abroad, and commercial policy at home, therefore became highly protectionist. Rich subsidies were offered to those who produced for the export market; high tariffs and other obstacles were imposed on imports. Nations like Britain forbade their colonies from trading with anyone else, lest their wealth leaked to adversaries such as France, Spain or the Netherlands. War was seen as a legitimate way of increasing the national wealth by plundering the wealth of other countries. At home, towns raised similar barriers against manufacturers and artisans from other towns, while trade associations – the guilds – strictly regulated their own professions in order to keep out competitors. Guilds even petitioned the monarch to outlaw labour-saving devices that threatened the livelihood of their members, and rewarded their business cronies by granting them monopolies on essential products like starch and salt.

This was *mercantilism* – a system designed for the benefit of producers rather than of consumers. It is often caricatured as early capitalism, because businesses were being created, and capital, manufacturing, markets and trade were all growing. But in nearly all other respects it was very different from the idea of capitalism. It was beset by controls and tariffs by which those in power sought to steer the nation's economic activity. Those controls in turn depended on the coercive power of the state being used for that purpose. It legitimised cronyism, theft and force. If capitalism existed anywhere, it existed only in the so-called *liberties*, outside the towns, where the rule of the guilds and civic authorities did not run, and where free commerce, innovation and new ideas could emerge.

Adam Smith dissected the mercantilist system in *The Wealth of Nations*. He pointed out that both buyers and sellers benefited from voluntary trade: they would not engage in it otherwise. The sellers may receive gold and silver, but the buyers get goods or services that they value more than the money they pay. Trade is not something we should resist: the more trade there is, the more value is created and the more wealth is spread to the citizens of all countries. Open competition promotes innovation and value for money. And the specialisation that is made possible by capital and markets leads to huge gains in productivity, which benefits everyone, particularly the poor. Yet all this can be stifled, Smith warned, by state power, particularly when that power is wielded on be-half of cronies and to protect the established producer interests.

Mercantilism, with its controls, subsidies, taxes, war-fare and primitive ideas on trade and value, was therefore certainly not the 'system of natural liberty' that today we call capitalism. But Adam Smith's arguments prevailed. By the 1860s, mercantilist controls were being replaced by lower taxes and deregulation. The result was a remarkable period of free trade, and the fastest economic growth Brit-ain had ever experienced.

The Industrial Revolution

When most people think of capitalism they perhaps think of the mills and factory towns of Britain's Industrial Rev-olution in the late eighteenth and early nineteenth centu-ries, and of the grim picture that authors such as Charles Dickens (1812–70), and indeed Marx, painted of them.

Certainly, the economy of this period was closer to the idea of capitalism than mercantilism ever was. It was a relatively free and low-tax economy, where multiple inventions transformed agriculture and manufacturing, where the new water and steam power technology drove the spinning and weaving mills that turned wool from England and raw cotton from America into cheap and high-quality clothing for export to the world.

Yet the Marxist–Dickensian account has greatly obscured the true nature and effects of these astonishing developments. Such critics see the origins of the Industrial Revolution in the late eighteenth-century Enclosure Act, which allowed landowners to fence off farmland. Peasant farmers, runs the argument, were consequently driven out of rural areas and into grim towns, where mill owners exploited them as cheap labour.

Yet this is a caricature. The enclosures were neither quick nor easy: each required Parliamentary approval, and objections had to be considered. A much stronger factor in the migration from rural to urban areas was that wages in the factory towns were higher, and rising much faster than they were on the land. Industrial innovation, water and steam power, specialisation and international trade vastly increased people's productivity, and their earnings along with it.

This was no tale of people being forced into urban poverty. By 1820, the average earnings of every income group in England were rising fast – including the poorest. Factory work also offered a far more reliable stream of income than people could expect from seasonal work on the land, with its variable harvests. Though millworkers' hours might have been long by our standards, they were no longer than the hours required to raise crops, while the labour itself was far less backbreaking, and sheltered from the extremes of the weather. In the towns, there were also shops and amenities, and far greater opportunities for social life, cultural activities and education. Housing was cramped, particularly as more children survived and families grew; but urban homes were drier, warmer, cleaner, more sanitary and better ventilated than the hovels of rural workers. The well-off metropolitan intelligentsia were shocked at how the urban poor lived – but few had any understanding at all of the rural poverty they had willingly left.

The very wealth that the towns created itself drove further improvements in working and living conditions, consolidated by new laws on child labour, hours, wages and housing standards – all of which would have been impossible in the age of subsistence farming. And those wages were going much further, given the huge drop in price and rise in quality of clothing and the many other products that the urban workers themselves were producing.

The state-managed economy

From around the 1880s, however, the relatively free economic environment that helped urban production to expand came under increasing intellectual pressure. Successes in the physical sciences led to a rising belief that social and economic life could be controlled rationally and scientifically. Urban communities allowed workers to come together and organise politically, demanding even stronger regulations on pay and conditions. Political tensions across Europe led to the re-emergence of protectionist, almost mercantilist, policies. Trade and commerce gradually became more regulated, and by the early twentieth century there were calls for governments to intervene in the operation of essential services such as railways, or even take over the running of whole industries.

In the 1930s, in the aftermath of the Great Depression, more countries opted for more of this nationalisation. A new wave of economists urged governments to increase their spending in the hope of kick-starting recovery, and thence to 'fine tune' their economies through tax, credit and monetary policies. By the 1960s, virtually all the superficially capitalist countries on the globe had in fact become mixed economies, with private and public enterprises existing side by side, the regulation of companies, employment and markets, 'indicative planning' by the authorities, protectionist trade barriers, and government management of the economy – hardly true to the principles of capitalism at all.

But this mixture brought its own problems. The wider effects of government policies were improperly understood. Government spending that was supposed to boost the economy in fact boosted bouts of runaway price rises that actually disrupted it. State-run industries, always able to fall back on taxpayers' money, became notoriously bad in terms of efficiency and customer service. Planners simply could not collect and process all the information they needed to run a complex economy. Economic policy, which was supposed to be rational, became politicised and fought over by vested interest groups. Labour disputes increased. Cronyism came to distort all production.

The scourge of corporatism

This cronyism is perhaps the prevailing form of economy today. Many people call it crony capitalism but it is better called crony socialism. It is a world away from capitalism in the sense of enterprise, innovation, productivity, free markets and competition, all driven by the demands of consumers. Rather, it is about firms with monopolistic ambitions using political influence to thwart all those things: an alliance of business and government that might pretend (and even believe itself) to be on the side of consumers, but is not.

Given the growth of governments over the last century, and their penetration into every part of economic life, plenty of commercial favours can be extracted from them. Governments can give out subsidies and tax breaks, raise or lower tariffs and trade barriers, make grants of land or money or monopolies, require new businesses to obtain permits to trade, or create regulations and pay-scales that are unaffordable to all except the established firms. They can tolerate collusion among those same firms, or even require them to get together in planning forums at which prices and production can be fixed: a kind of state-sponsored cartel. And in the name of preventing crises or preserving jobs, governments are easily persuaded to bail out businesses that are badly managed, who cannot match the price or quality of foreign competitors, or whose product is simply no longer in demand from consumers.

So it is that banks, airlines, builders, manufacturers, energy suppliers, phone companies, media firms, pharmaceutical companies, carmakers, supermarkets, landowners, wind turbine engineers, bus and train companies, importers and many others – though nominally private firms – are dependent on governments for favours, subsidies, tax breaks, permits and competition-choking regulations.

Even if the original intentions of all this were noble – to promote economic stability, safeguard jobs, improve amenities, protect the environment and so on – the effects of this government largesse are malign. It draws businesses into politics. It encourages what economists call *rent seeking* – lobbying for privileges that secure easy profits, stemming either from the public purse or from regulations that reduce competition. The larger the government becomes, the greater are the potential benefits from such lobbying – and indeed, from corruption and cronyism. The more the existing producer interests are indulged, the bigger the incumbents grow, the more the government relies on them in shaping future regulation, and the more that potential competitors and new technologies are squeezed out. The diverse interests of consumers are ignored, with political debate becoming monopolised by the lobbying of producers, whose interests are more concentrated, and who have more money and more professional skill to lobby more effectively than individual consumers.

Yet this cronyism is common all over the world, especially in South East Asia, where the term 'crony capitalism' was coined, and where governments commonly support 'leader' companies in each sector, protecting them with regulations and tariff walls. To them, the benefits of having a few large and strong companies that can compete internationally are obvious. But they forget the opportunity cost: the fact that the capital, personnel and other resources employed by these big companies might be used more productively elsewhere. Indeed, given that governments cannot possibly spot every opportunity that might be seen by countless individuals, it is almost certain that they could be.

Such commercial privilege is possible only where governments are prepared to use coercive force. It is not possible in a free society where governments use force only to protect individual rights. But the fact that cronyism is so common indicates how many countries around the world are now free only in name.

Creating a capitalism for the future

It is hard to describe any of these economic systems as capitalism in any true sense, though of course many people try to, using sleight of hand or conflation to burden the ideal of capitalism with many practical blemishes that are neither exclusive nor essential to it. The challenge for capitalism's supporters is to separate the core idea from the conflations and confusions, and to go on to create in practice an economic arrangement that is closer to their vision of capitalism, with all its economic, social and moral benefits.

That, of course, means dissolving state-owned enterprises and cutting down the taxes, subsidies, tariffs and regulations that thwart competition and fuel cronyism and corporatism. It means limiting the state to protecting people's rights and economic freedoms, rather than violating them. It means a separation between state and economic life.

This is not an easy agenda to achieve in an unlimited democracy, where more and more decisions are made through the political process, giving the majority the supposed right to impose all sorts of economic policies on the minority. That is not democracy but populism, backed up by the coercive power of the state, and it is why the founders of the United States put such strict limits on their government, and separated its powers between different institutions. Yet even there, power has become centralised and concentrated.

These are perfect conditions for cronyism, and very difficult ones for capitalism, as rightly understood. To replace cronyism, with all its faults, by capitalism, with all its benefits, would seem to require a systematic rethink of the limitations of and the limits on the political process.

9 GREAT THINKERS ON CAPITALISM

The School of Salamanca (the 'Scholastics')

Property, supply and demand, interest

Between the fifteenth and seventeenth centuries, Spanish clerics made a number of breakthroughs in the understanding of economics, enabling capitalism to be reconciled with the Christian scriptures that so often seemed to criticise it. For example: the first of these so-called *Scholastics*, Francisco de Vitoria (1483–1546), was consulted by merchants who were worried how God and the Church would view their trade. Vitoria considered the matter, concluding that the free movement of people, goods and ideas was part of Nature, which was God's creation. The merchant trade was therefore not wicked, but in fact served the general good.

The Biblical scriptures were also critical of usury – charging interest on loans. But in the Scholastics' time, the Renaissance had brought many opportunities for entrepreneurial activity, and loan finance was becoming very important to the conduct of business and trade. Fortunately, the Scholastics found many ways to justify loan interest.

Borrowers benefited, they noted, which was good; interest was a payment – a premium – for the risk if a loan went bad; there was an 'opportunity cost' to the lender, since there were many other potential uses for the same money; and money itself was a good, you should pay to borrow it, just like renting any other good.

Scholastics also defended private property. It had the benefit of stimulating economic activity and therefore prosperity, they argued. People also took better care of property that they owned themselves, rather than shared in common with others, meaning that God's creations were better cherished. Individuals, they concluded, had a right to own and benefit from their property – except in emergencies, when they had a duty to share with those in need.

The Scholastics even identified the importance of supply and demand. They saw that precious metals commanded a higher price in countries where they were scarce. The 'just price' of a good was not simply the cost of its production and transport – how could the same bale of linen be worth more if it was carried expensively over land rather than cheaply by sea? The price depended on the interplay of supply and demand – provided that market was kept free and open.

Adam Smith (1723–90)

The benefits of specialisation, commerce and free trade

The Scottish philosopher turned economist Adam Smith is best known for his book *The Wealth of Nations* (1776), in which he weaved his own ideas and those of many other authors into a new, systematic and recognisably modern approach to economics. The book attacked the prevailing system of *mercantilism*, which measured a nation's wealth by its stockpiles of gold and silver, and which used subsidies to maximise export sales and tariffs to block import purchases. Smith pointed out that both sides benefit from trade. Indeed, neither would bother to trade unless it made them better off. True, the sellers get the cash: but the buyers get goods that they value more than the price they pay.

Smith concluded that what made a country rich was not its holdings of cash, but the magnitude of its production, trade and commerce – what we now call gross national product or GDP.

We can greatly increase that product, he observed, by specialisation, which allows us to become skilled and more productive – even more so if we invest in specialist capital goods such as tools and equipment. By exchanging our specialist products with others, at home or abroad, we all gain from the boost to productivity that is brought by this specialisation and capital investment.

Where there is free trade and competition, Smith argued, markets steer effort and resources to the most productive users and steer finished products to those whose demand for them is strongest. It is a highly cooperative system, but it works only where there is freedom of action, free trade and open competition. Smith was very critical of crony capitalism, in which producers would pressure politicians for monopolies or special favours.

Government, he concluded, should not intervene in economic life, apart from maintaining the structure that allows it to function.

David Ricardo (1772–1823)

Comparative advantage and productive efficiency

A successful London stockbroker and speculator (it was said he made £1m gambling on a British victory at Waterloo), Ricardo started thinking about economics after reading Adam Smith's *The Wealth of Nations*. He went on to make major advances in the theory of rents, wages, profits, taxation and value.

On trade policy, he rejected protectionist measures such as the Corn Laws, which restricted imports of wheat; and he developed the 'theory of comparative costs' (now called the *theory of comparative advantage*), for which he is best known. Countries, he said, could make themselves better off by specialising in what they could produce relatively cheaper – in terms of all the other things that they could produce – than other countries. Even if a country could produce everything more cheaply than another, it would still be better off specialising in those goods where it has a comparative – and not necessarily an absolute – advantage.

To give a modern example: a famous movie star may happen to be a better cook than the film studio chef. Yet despite that *absolute* advantage over the chef, the studio is still better off keeping its star on set, exploiting the comparative advantage of their talent and celebrity, rather than sending them off to the kitchen. This principle remains one of the key foundations of the argument for free trade.

Ludwig von Mises (1881–1973)

The nature of capital; critique of socialism; the benefits of laissez-faire

Mises became the leading figure in the 'Austrian School' of economists, which emphasised the complexity of economic phenomena and how the values and actions of millions of individuals were critical to the overall result. What was important about capital, for instance, was not its total value but its structure – exactly what capital goods people invested in, and how those capital goods worked productively together. This structure was delicate: for example, inept interest-rate policy distorted markets, inducing people to invest in the wrong things – malinvestment – leading to failures and losses.

Where markets were completely eliminated, as under communism, rational investment became impossible. Without prices, no one could ever calculate which of many possible production processes would be the most cost-effective. Inevitably, resources would be invested in the wrong processes, leading to waste and inefficiency, and the mistakes would accumulate over time because there would be no market pressure to eliminate them.

Mises made a robust case for laissez-faire, arguing that as soon as governments started to hamper the market system with controls and regulations, they set off tides of dislocations (such as surpluses and shortages) that spread from market to market, like ripples in a pond, distorting one market after another. In trying to limit the damage, governments then were then drawn to intervene further, which made things even worse.

F. A. Hayek (1899–1992)

Spontaneous order; critique of planning; market coordination

A student of Ludwig von Mises, the Vienna-born Hayek collaborated with him on research into boom–bust business cycles, concluding that these were caused by central banks setting interest rates too low, which encouraged excessive borrowing and spending. But low rates also discouraged saving, and when lenders' funds dried up, investors faced a credit crunch, their over-optimistic investments had to be abandoned, and capital and jobs were lost.

One of Hayek's key insights was the concept of *spontaneous order*. Human and animal societies show obvious regularities. Yet nobody planned how bees live or how humans use language. Such orders arose naturally and persisted because they were useful. Often we cannot even articulate the rules (such as the rules of grammar) that underpin them. And since we do not fully understand how such natural orders work, it is a conceit to imagine we can do better – that we can wave away the price mechanism by imposing wage and price controls, for example, or improve on the free market through central economic planning.

In Hayek's view, the economic planner cannot even access the information that would be necessary for such a task, because that information is dispersed, local, partial, rapidly changing, specific, personal and hard to transmit. Yet markets deal with all this information, from moment to moment, at dispersed local levels. No planner needs to decide how resources should be used: prices provide the simple signals that steer them automatically to their most valued uses. Market orders are therefore far more efficient, and can grow much larger, than planned systems.

Milton Friedman (1912–2006)

The importance of sound money; the costs of regulation

Friedman was a particularly able and persuasive communicator of liberal ideas. Through his book *Capitalism and Freedom* (1962) and his TV series and book *Free to Choose* (1980) – both written with his wife Rose – millions of people came to learn about the potential of free markets, open trade, freedom and capitalism.

In 1946, Friedman collaborated on a pungent repudiation of rent controls. Such policies, he observed, made landlords less willing to maintain and rent out their property, reducing both the quality and supply of available accommodation. He also studied the regulation and licensing of professions (such as doctors, lawyers and accountants), concluding that it benefits not the public, but the practitioners. By restricting competition, he found, licensing forces customers to pay more for poorer service.

Friedman is best known for his work on monetary policy and its effect on inflation – a major problem in the late twentieth century. He criticised the mainstream view that governments could control inflation by adjusting their taxing and spending, arguing that they instead had to control the quantity of money in circulation. But monetary policy was a very blunt tool, so governments should simply set up a sound framework and give up their constant economic meddling.

James M. Buchanan (1919–2013) and Gordon Tullock (1922–2014)

Critique of political decision making

Buchanan and Tullock developed the Public Choice School of economics, which challenged the idea that market failure justified government intervention. More often, they explained, government failure made things even worse because the policymaking process was riddled with self-interest and exploitation.

The rot starts with elections, which Buchanan and Tullock pointed out were not tests of the 'public interest' but contests of competing interests. Under capitalism, people can have whichever different products they choose. In elections, the majority make the choices for everyone – and can also use the power of the state to help them exploit the minority, which producers under capitalism cannot.

Elections, too, are dominated by special-interest groups that have a strong specific interest in the outcome, rather than by the general public, whose interests are more diffused and moderate. And even the most public-spirited politician needs to make concessions to these interest groups in order to be elected. Policy becomes focused on what is expedient, not what is rational.

Moreover, to get their measures through the legislature, politicians generally have to make further adjustments to secure the support of their colleagues and other legislators. They may well have to strike 'You vote for my measure and I will vote for yours' deals with them – meaning that everyone ends up with more legislation than anyone really wanted. Lastly, the officials who implement the legislation that comes out of this irrational process have their own particular interests to pursue: for example, they may seek to expand their personal bureaucratic empires by making the rules highly complex, requiring more personnel to manage them.

Capitalism may not be perfect, Buchanan and Tullock concluded: but nor should we be dewy-eyed about the alternative.

Gary Becker (1930–2014)

Human capital; economic solutions to social problems

A student of Milton Friedman, the American economist Gary Becker broke new ground by applying economic concepts to many different kinds of social issues, including the motivations of criminals, discrimination against minorities, and immigration. However, he is best known for his work on *human capital* – though he did not coin the phrase himself.

Human capital is the qualities, knowledge and skills that make individuals more productive. It includes investments in education and training, but also includes useful values such as punctuality and diligence, and even good health. Becker identified two kinds of human capital: *specific* and *general*. Specific human capital is knowledge relevant to a particular business, such as how to use its proprietary software. Firms pay for employees to acquire this knowledge because they know that, were the employee to leave, the information would be useless to competitors. General human capital is knowledge that can be used anywhere, such as keyboard skills. Firms are unwilling to pay for such transferable skills, so people generally have to acquire them at their own expense.

Becker's approach provides other interesting insights. For example, he suggests that one reason why people today spend longer in education than previous generations is that they are living longer – lengthening and increasing the potential gains they can make from having transferable skills. Technological advances have also made it more profitable to acquire advanced knowledge and high-tech skills because that can make them much more productive and more highly valued. The human capital idea even helps explain why more women are in education than ever before. It is not just a matter of sociological change, but because home automation has liberated women to pursue their own careers.

There is one last, but vitally important, conclusion. As technology changes faster and faster, says Becker, there is now more need for lifetime learning that enables people to develop new skills and keep their human capital refreshed.

Israel Kirzner (1930–)

The role of entrepreneurship; the importance of dynamic effects

Born in London, Kirzner studied under Ludwig von Mises in New York. Like Mises, he argued that the standard 'static equilibrium' models obscured the *dynamic* nature of economics. Economic activity never settled in some perfect balance: on the contrary, individuals were constantly correcting their plans and adjusting their actions in response to the similarly changing actions of others. This dynamic process kept their actions in constant – though not perfect – coordination.

Kirzner explained that entrepreneurship had a vital role in driving, maintaining and improving this coordination. Entrepreneurship is the process in which individuals (not necessarily professional entrepreneurs, but ordinary people too) spot gaps and mismatches in the market and then act to fill and correct them. For example, someone might spot that a new material means certain products can be made lighter or more durable; another might spot that a new office development will fuel demand for a nearby coffee shop; another might believe that a popular local bakery could succeed as a national chain. They may act on these hunches solely because they stand to make entrepreneurial profit for themselves: but in doing so, they help the coordination of human economic actions by bringing production into better alignment with the public's various needs and wants.

This in turn shows that economic adjustment and co-ordination relies heavily on the local knowledge of market conditions that different people might have. But this is simply forgotten in the 'perfect information' idea of mainstream economics. It also reminds us that we must have the right policies, institutions and open markets in place for this entrepreneurial spirit to thrive.

Deirdre McCloskey (1942–)

Liberal values and economic growth

McCloskey was born male but transitioned to female at the age of 53. Already known (as Donald McCloskey) for work on price theory and other subjects, her major impact came later, as the result of her study of the economic history of Britain. She concluded that the massive economic growth experienced over the last two centuries can be explained not so much by capital or institutions but by the spread of liberal ideas – specifically, 'bourgeois values'.

McCloskey underlines the sheer scale of recent economic growth. In 1800 the average person earned the equivalent of only a few dollars a day. Today, average earnings are tens of times greater. Given that the world population has grown sevenfold since 1800, that is a huge increase in wealth. Nor is it merely material enrichment: with increasing wealth, longevity and literacy, it is an intellectual and cultural enrichment too.

This *Great Enrichment* – the biggest leap in prosperity since the dawn of agriculture, but much bigger – began around 1860. It is not fully explained by the steady economic growth of Britain since the Black Death in the fourteenth century, nor even by the Industrial Revolution that began in the late eighteenth century, nor by Britain's institutions and rule of law. Only ideas, she insists, can change things so much so fast. The Great Enrichment stemmed from the spread of 'bourgeois liberalism' that allowed ordinary people, for the first time, to enjoy liberty, dignity and prosperity. For centuries, commerce had been thought venal and demeaning: but writers like John Locke and Adam Smith defended the virtues of freedom, trade, the accumulation of wealth and capital, and the dignity and self-esteem it gave to ordinary citizens. Suddenly, there was nothing to hold back the creative genius of a free people.

10 CRITICS AND CRITICISMS

Ironically, people like the American filmmaker Michael Moore (1954–), the Korean economist Ha-Joon Chang (1962–), the Canadian activist Naomi Klein (1970–) and the French writer Thomas Piketty (1971–) have made themselves wealthy through their criticism of capitalism. It seems that if there is a demand for their ideas, capitalism rewards even its own critics – unlike other systems, which typically stamp criticism out.

Equally there are academics, teachers, writers and artists who feel that capitalism undervalues them, and that in a more just society, they would have greater status and authority. But they forget that it is not capitalism that puts a value on their work, but other people. And who is to say that other people's valuations of them should not be respected?

Whatever the source, however, there are many valid criticisms of capitalism that its supporters must address: moral criticisms, concerns about the structure of capitalist economies, criticisms of corporate power, and geopolitical concerns.

Moral criticisms

Equality versus prosperity. Capitalist societies are remark-ably equal, but as people exchange money for goods and services, there will inevitably be changes in their financial holdings (albeit balanced by the enjoyment of what they buy). The only way to preserve financial equality would be constant redistribution.

Many of the statistics on financial inequality are misleading, because they focus on incomes before tax is deducted and welfare benefits are paid. When tax and benefits are considered, equality is actually very similar across the world, with the bottom 10 per cent of earners getting around 40 per cent of the median income. The stat-istics also obscure the effects of age and mobility: younger people tend to be less wealthy, since they have yet to build up their human and physical capital; while immigrants and others with few skills take low-paid jobs but regard them as stepping stones to better-paid ones. Such progres-sion is natural in any system.

Some critics, seeing the impossibility of complete equality, advocate very high inheritance taxes, so that wealth does not simply trickle down to unproductive indi-viduals, and everyone has to start life on a roughly equal footing. But there are many moral and other objections. For example, it defies human nature, because humans have a powerful desire to provide for their children; some people live longer than others, allowing them to trans-fer more to their children while still alive; people would squander their money rather than see it taxed away on death, leading to lower investment and lower future prosperity; family-owned firms would disappear. And in any case, inherited wealth, as we have seen, is not permanent.

While nearly everyone supports equal treatment and equality of opportunity in principle, they are remarkably unwilling to sacrifice their own prosperity for greater equality. It is said that money cannot buy happiness, but all the evidence is that it does. The problem we need to address is not equality of incomes but sufficient incomes: do people have enough to live on decently?

Capitalism and greed. The criticism that capitalism is based on greed stems from confusing greed and self-interest: if providers were really greedy, their customers would desert them. And why level the accusation of 'greed' only at business? Businesses may be hungry for profit, but customers are equally hungry for savings, while workers are hungry for higher pay. Yet we rarely hear criticism of 'greedy' customers and workers.

Except occasionally: for example, critics say that capitalism encourages greed in everyone, creating resistance against taxes that are needed for vital public services. But questioning taxes is no bad thing: most public services (such as healthcare and education) can be provided privately in the market or supported (like cultural and welfare programmes) through civil society. And though taxation may be necessary, it is a necessary evil. After all, it is taken from people by force; it is spent on things (like prisons, the military or abortions) that some taxpayers deeply oppose; it encourages monopoly state provision, which is less efficient and provides less choice; it induces lobbying and cronyism as people vie to get subsidies and favours for themselves; and it creates perverse incentives – for example, income tax makes work less rewarding, inheritance taxes discourage saving and investment.

Materialism and consumerism. Another moral criticism is that capitalism promotes materialism and 'excess' consumption.

The argument has a strange lineage. Early critics of capitalism said that it was not working, and that rational planning would raise living standards faster: but events proved this wrong. More recently, therefore, the criticism has been that capitalism works too well, allowing people to satisfy their wants to 'excess' and consume fripperies, diverting them from important social objectives. But what counts as 'excess' is a matter of opinion – which is a poor basis for public policy, particularly one that would mean using force to stifle such consumption.

There are two other weaknesses in this argument. First, we have no moral authority for preventing people from producing and consuming what they value, even if we do not value it ourselves – and certainly no moral authority for forcing them to act in accordance with our values, however virtuous we might suppose them. That would breach their rights to choice and self-determination.

Second, the main reason we adopt capitalism is precisely that it is so good at producing economic goods. We do not adopt it to produce *social* outcomes such as equality or solidarity. It is the wrong tool for that job, and we can hardly blame it for that. It does in fact produce some happy social outcomes such as peace and general prosperity – but that is just a bonus.

Cost-cutting and quality. Many critics think that competition forces producers to cut costs to the bone, leaving consumers with cheap but shoddy goods. Things, they complain, are not made to last – which is irrational and a false economy.

In fact, the competitive pressure on producers is to meet customers' demands, whatever those might be. People might demand quality in some cases, and cheapness in others. For example, if fashions change quickly, there is no point in producing expensive clothes that soon go out of style. Likewise with personal electronics that might soon be made obsolete by new technologies. On the other hand, for durable goods (like lawnmowers or grand pianos) where fashion or technological change is not very important, consumers may well prefer better-built products to cheap ones.

In all cases, it depends on the consumer: older and richer buyers may prefer higher-quality but higher-cost goods, while younger and poorer customers may prefer lower-quality but more affordable ones. Who is to deny them that choice?

People make poor choices. Some critics object that many people make bad choices, such as savings plans they do not understand or goods that do not meet their need. They argue that new products, particularly financial products, should be strictly regulated – or even banned until their full effects are known.

But banning new products on the grounds that people might make mistakes in buying them is a sure way to kill off innovation and progress. Future generations who would benefit from this progress lose out. There may be a case for some simple and general protections, such as cooling-off periods for complex savings products. Much regulation, however, is pointless. Nobody checks a licence: they ask friends and neighbours whom they recommend.

None of us (not even a regulator) can anticipate everything, so we buy products on the basis of the best information we have about them. Most people are perfectly capable of making their own choices on that basis. They also know their own needs far better than some distant official: regulators cannot know what particular motives prompt individuals to buy what they do – so what right or reason do they have to stop them? If we bail people out when they make mistakes, we merely encourage them to be careless; if we deny them the power to choose, we turn them into ciphers. It is more effective, and more moral, for people to accept the consequences of their choices.

Structual criticisms

Anarchy of production. Many critics see capitalist production as inefficient, irrational and anarchic. For example, different firms produce similar products, and have to waste money advertising them: a single large-scale producer would be more efficient, and advertising would be unnecessary. Also, resources could be used, and production structured, more rationally and less wastefully if production were properly planned, rather than being left to the random nature of capitalist production.

But such criticisms forget that competition makes capitalism highly *dynamic*. Firms do *not* all produce the same things, but try to make their own offers more attractive to customers by constantly improving them and cutting out wasteful costs. As experience shows, a single producer would have far less incentive to improve either its product or its efficiency.

There is actually plenty of planning in capitalism: individuals and firms make plans all the time. Those plans get constant and instant feedback from the daily decisions of customers on what they will or will not buy, and producers quickly adjust their plans accordingly. If they make a mistake, it is only they who suffer. But things are quite different when a nation's entire production is planned. Such huge schemes are slow to put into effect and to change; there is less feedback because consumers have less choice; so there is less dynamism and progress. And if the plan proves mistaken, the whole nation suffers.

Unproductive speculation. Many critics object to the financial speculation that exists under capitalism: betting on shares or currency prices, futures markets and all the rest. This, they say, produces nothing but absorbs a great deal of time, energy and money.

In fact, speculation is a sign of a lively economy and capital market, and speculators *do* produce something of value. Since production is specialised, speculators must make themselves highly knowledgeable on just a few firms or a single sector if they are to match their competitors. Their informed decisions on where to invest or disinvest are therefore a valuable indicator of the health and prospects of those firms and sectors, helping other people to make better decisions on where to commit their own money. By cutting the risk of investing, this encourages greater investment, capital creation and therefore productive efficiency – and it speeds resources into their most productive uses.

Undemocratic production. Another criticism is that under capitalism, production is organised to benefit owners, when in fact it should be structured to benefit the public and other stakeholders. Production should therefore be brought under democratic control – so it could be run in the long-term interest of the nation, not the short-term interest of owners.

Unfortunately, 'democratic' control means political control – with all of the problems of politics, including the power of pressure groups and the self-interest of voters, politicians and officials. An economy run politically, for the benefit of the stakeholders, means one run for the benefit of current stakeholders – who have a clear interest in maintaining current practices rather than let progress disrupt things. And who is more short-termist than politicians, always looking to the next election? Owners, by contrast, do benefit if they promote the long-term strength of their business – which will attract capital and raise its value.

Corporate power

Big corporations. Much criticism of capitalism focuses on the power of large corporations. They are seen as powerful bodies that can manipulate politicians, public opinion and consumers' choices, extract regulation and tax favours from the state, and create monopolies.

But monopolies and big corporations are not an inevitable part of capitalism. Under capitalist competition, the only way for companies to stay big is to keep on serving the public. Even the largest company can be challenged by another, or by smaller companies eating away at different parts of its business. The only way they can create monopolies is to thwart competition by tax or regulatory favours from the state. This is not capitalism, but cronyism.

The blame for that rests firmly on the state. The state has power to tax and make laws and regulations; it can even can throw you in jail or make you fight in wars. Businesses cannot. However much people complain about the power of large companies, the state is where real power resides. We need politicians to promote competition, not serve the interests of the large and the established producers.

Management versus ownership. Some critics argue that large public corporations are dysfunctional because management has become separated from ownership. Managers have become unrestrained, powerful and overpaid.

But the division of ownership and management is merely another example of the division of labour. Certainly, the owners (i.e. shareholders) of companies should have the power to control their managers, though bad company law has eroded that power in many countries – another case of politics disrupting the smooth workings of capitalism.

Also, the larger a business, the more skilled the manager that is needed to run it. There are very few people who can run a world-class international corporation, so not surprisingly, they are well paid. But not necessarily *over*paid: when a good chief executive decides to leave, the value of a company can plummet. It should be for the owners to decide whether managers are worth the money, not politicians who have other, political, motives.

Global relationships

Multinationals. Few enterprises attract more criticism than multinational corporations. Critics accuse them of lobbying for special protections, shifting costs between countries to save taxes and moving their most polluting processes to poorer countries. World markets, they argue, are undermined by big capital, and multinationals, some as big as whole countries, act more like imperial nations than market players.

But it is governments and cronyism that allow companies to grow on this scale. And countries have different tax regimes precisely because some wish to attract growth-boosting business and capital. Multinationals have in fact made huge investments in poorer countries, bringing capital that makes their industries more productive, opening up work opportunities and raising wages. It may be that some of the work is more arduous, and some of the processes less clean, than people in rich countries would choose for themselves; but the alternative is that these countries' development is slowed, their hope of affording easier and cleaner production is postponed, and their people live in poverty for longer.

As for imperialism, multinationals and global markets have actually promoted world peace. Their investments in emerging economies have helped take billions out of poverty and create a thriving middle class that has everything to gain from preserving peace and the trade that peace makes possible.

McDonaldisation. Nevertheless, some critics argue that with the richer countries' investment comes cultural imperialism too, with Western brands, lifestyles and practices swamping local ones.

But the truth is that globalisation has actually promoted the spread of more diverse goods and services. Now that large parts of Eastern Europe and South East Asia are no longer closed off from the West, both sides can enjoy more products from more countries than ever before. The rising wealth that trade has given the emerging economies brings more of them to the richer countries as students or as tourists, carrying their values and culture with them. The result is not cultural imperialism, but diversity and choice.

Job protection. It is often said that emerging economies need special protection so that they can grow their 'infant' industries and become economically strong. That means controls, import tariffs and export subsidies that would prevent richer countries undercutting them.

But in fact the greatest problem in poorer countries is lack of capital; and their opening up to foreign investment is the quickest way to get it. The new capital makes them more productive – able to produce goods and services that can compete with any in the world, and helping local people pursue their own ambitions.

Protectionism is possible only in non-free countries, where states can force taxpayers to subsidise favoured industries, or can impose tariffs and quotas against importers. But markets are now global: countries gain from being a part of them, and cannot develop – or even keep up – behind protectionist walls.

Confounding the cronies

A number of capitalism's critics argue that there is no such thing as free markets. There is always lobbying and collusion, so there need to be strong regulations and rules to make capitalism work tolerably well.

But capitalism's supporters also reject collusion and cronyism, and see them as not unique to capitalism. Indeed, they are more rife in socialist systems. And the rules that allow markets to function – of justice and the rights to own and trade property freely – are far simpler and more general than the detailed regulations that the critics propose.

Rather, government should focus on its key roles of protecting individual rights and liberties, not trying to run the economy: a kind of division between economy and state. The sad lesson of history is that public officials are neither wiser nor more ethical than ordinary people. Indeed, state power attracts the worst in those who would deploy it, and enables them to make bigger mistakes.

11 THE FUTURE OF CAPITALISM

Capitalism has many strengths, and there are many opportunities for it to spread peace and prosperity around the world. But it also has weaknesses and faces threats that could weaken it further – disrupting its delicate mechanisms, distorting its effects and undermining its support among the public.

Strengths

Prosperity. The main argument for capitalism, even in today's highly regulated form, is that it rapidly boosts prosperity, particularly for the poorest. The recent globalisation of world markets and capital has lifted billions of people out of abject poverty, increasing incomes and wealth, and bringing better healthcare, greater longevity, falling infant mortality, increasing literacy and numeracy (especially among females) and many other human benefits.

In addition, access to world capital has made the businesses of the emerging economies more productive. That allows local people to enjoy better, cheaper and more plentiful local products, and for their incomes to go further. Greater productivity also makes it easier for new businesses to succeed, reducing the risk of starting new enterprises and encouraging innovation and progress.

Freeing minds. By making production easier and more productive, by supplying goods that liberate human beings from drudgery, and by creating wealth that saves people from worrying about their everyday existence, capitalism frees people to apply their minds to the things they value and use their intelligence to solve their other problems. And freeing lots of different brains to think about how we live of course promotes progress too. Different people put forward different plans that can be tested in the markets for goods – and for ideas too. We can then build on what works, and drop what does not, far more rapidly than if we were committed to some single national plan.

Many personal utopias. Capitalism is pluralist. As Brennan says, capitalism does not promote a utopia – it promotes many utopias. Different people can pursue different ambitions and vocations just as they choose. They do not have to wait for the government to assign them their role in the collective project. They can make their own heaven, without stopping anyone else from making theirs. All they have to do is to get along with others – they do not have to oppress them as Marx suggested the bourgeois classes did. Capitalism allows many different flowers to bloom.

Human nature. Capitalism is also rooted in human nature. People have a strong attachment to their own property: their possessions are important to them and have a meaning for them beyond their material worth. Our ideas of justice are equally deep, as is our commitment to people honouring the promises they make. People also want to be free to live and act as they choose, while living peacefully with others. And they want to better their own condition, and that of their families. These are the very foundations of capitalism. So it is no wonder that, even in the most ruthless collectivist countries, people try to build and protect their own property, and markets break into existence at every opportunity.

Weaknesses

Statism and cronyism. It is hard to defend what is commonly called 'capitalism' today. What passes for 'capitalism' in most parts of the world are in fact mixed economies in which private enterprises are highly taxed and highly regulated, where half or more of the national income is in government hands, and where state enterprises have monopolies or near-monopolies in important sectors including healthcare, education, utilities, rail transport and mail delivery. Often they are crony economies in which large businesses boost their economic power by extracting favours from politicians, sometimes in return for financial support.

However, it is equally hard to defend the 'socialism' that has prevailed in countries such as Soviet Russia, Mao's China, North Korea or Cuba – with their lack of accountability and democracy, and with their dictatorships, party elites, purges and famines that have taken the lives of perhaps a hundred million people.

The difference is that cronyism is not an inevitable part of capitalism, whereas these evils are an inevitable part of socialism. That is because capitalism is based on the principle of individual freedom and voluntary exchange. Socialism, by contrast, requires the existence of a political power that directs all economic activity. In capitalism, people do not have to agree: they can go about their own business and consume their own preferred mix of goods, without others having to agree with their choices. Socialism, however, presumes a collective goal, and collective means to achieve it, which people must agree on. Those who disagree must necessarily be forced to participate in the collective enterprise.

While capitalism rests on diversity and choice, therefore, socialism rests on conformity and power. But conformity is no friend of progress, while power corrupts even the most public spirited of individuals – and attracts those who are most ruthless in using it. One can imagine a 'pure' capitalism in which enterprises prosper only by serving customers in open competition, and are not supported by crony favours from the state. But one cannot imagine a 'pure' socialism in which everyone happily agrees to participate in the collective enterprise without some apparatus of state power to force them.

Business hypocrisy. But the power that enables politicians to grant favours to cronies explains why those in business are some of capitalism's weakest defenders, or even greatest enemies. Business corporations rarely support competition in their own sector. On the contrary, they call for regulations to restrict competition – often claiming that they are saving the public from dangerous 'cowboy' operators. Though they profess support for 'capitalism', they are adroit at arguing for the grants, subsidies, reliefs and other favours that politicians have within their gift.

The inability (or unwillingness) of business people to explain the public benefits of entrepreneurship and free markets is surely a huge weakness of capitalism, and a huge threat to it. By muddling capitalism with cronyism, such supposed champions do the cause no favours. The idea of capitalism is hard enough to understand already: the immediate benefits of interventions are easy to grasp, but not the long-term advantages of leaving markets and competition to work; and few people realise how delicate the market order is, and how wildly it can be thrown out of gear by even small political interventions.

False explanations. Moreover, since the reality in most developed economies is a mixed economy, it is hard for people to discern which events are caused by capitalism itself and which are caused by the political interventions that distort it. For example, nearly all politicians and most ordinary people imagine that the 2007/8 financial crash was caused by capitalism and the 'greedy bankers' it created. But supporters of capitalism retort that the crisis was actually fuelled by decades of low interest rates and loose monetary policy, and sparked by (well-intended but mistaken) US government regulations that forced banks to lend to poor families who they knew were bad credit risks – triggering the subprime mortgage disaster that brought down several financial institutions. They would also warn that governments' response to the crisis – to bail out the banks, create yet more money and reduce borrowing costs even further – merely prolongs the agony, producing economic stagnation. The right solution, they say, is to fix the banks by exposing them to competition, adopt sustainable monetary and credit policies, and let markets work to restore a sound economy.

The common explanations of the financial crash are therefore in error. But the events of 2007/8, the mistaken remedies applied, and the long period of low growth that followed, has created a widespread disillusionment with capitalism and free markets – bringing calls for yet more controls, regulations and other government interventions. Undoubtedly, this has all left the idea of capitalism seriously weakened.

Opportunities

The spread of capitalism. Nevertheless, capitalism itself continues to spread. Though once it seemed that communism would eventually cover the entire globe, today there are few parts of the world where capitalist ideas and practices have not penetrated. After the fall of the Soviet Union in the early 1990s, much of Asia, Eastern Europe and Africa threw themselves into the world trade network, and instituted reforms that allowed people to build their own businesses and trade more freely. That in turn has created a new middle class of people who run or work in capitalist enterprises, and who thirst for more of that same freedom and prosperity. With yet more markets opening up, plus the advances in global communications and transportation, this change is sure to accelerate. Politicians may worry about free trade taking domestic jobs, but all economists recognize its benefits: and now the vast majority of the world's population rely on capitalism and trade for the cheap and high-quality goods they can now enjoy.

Empowering the poor. Ensuring that the very poorest can participate fully in this development is both a challenge and an opportunity. Though people in poorer countries tend to save more, for example, their assets are not capital: indeed, their savings are often kept, unproductively, in cash. And as the Peruvian economist Hernando de Soto Polar (1941–) noted, some of the world's poorest build homes where they can, but without legitimate title, and run businesses and shops without obtaining the detailed licences required by the state. Since their homes and businesses have no legal standing, they cannot use them as collateral for loans and contracts, so can never grow their enterprises or achieve real financial security. However, states can help these people to prosper by issuing them title in their land and making regulation simpler and more realistic – turning their savings into productive capital and giving them a real stake in their country's economy.

No geographical or moral limits. There are no natural limits to the expansion of capitalism and new markets. Innovation continues to build on innovation, creating new opportunities for entrepreneurs to supply people's wants and needs better, cheaper, faster and to even more remote locations across even greater distances. Nobody knows where such freedom and progress will take us – which must depress the pessimists and planners, but excite the individualists and optimists who make up the greater part of humankind.

Nor do the opportunities stop at material benefits. The values of ownership, independence, freedom, peace and the rejection of force that are part of the capitalist package are also strengthened by the spread of free markets and trade. That has to be a moral gain that advances the human spirit.

Threats

Intellectuals. Perhaps the greatest threat to capitalism comes from intellectuals. Their motives may be public spirited, or not: perhaps they feel undervalued by the market, or fancy themselves running a new economic order, or do not trust others to make rational choices. Either way, the public and politicians still generally regard intellectuals as informed and wise, accept their criticisms of capitalism, and conclude that it needs serious repair.

But intellectuals rarely understand the nature and intricate workings of capitalism, and often have little personal experience of it. Too often, therefore, they imagine its problems, misdiagnose the causes and apply the wrong remedies.

Textbook errors. Many intellectuals, for example, remain steeped in the textbook model of 'perfect competition', which supposes large numbers of suppliers selling identical goods at identical prices. So they suppose that any variation in prices or in market share must be a fault. They take the rapid growth of a supermarket chain, for example, as a sign that the market must be 'imperfect' – rather than a sign that consumers simply prefer what it offers. The same supermarket cutting prices is taken as 'predatory practice' rather than an attempt to win customers in a rapidly changing market. As a result, they propose to restore the mythical 'perfect competition' by limiting the growth of firms or controlling their prices – killing off the very forces that make markets so dynamic. They do not realise that competition works only because economic life is imperfect, with firms trying to fill the gaps that arise, and jostling to offer something different, better and cheaper – not products that are identical to everyone else's.

Populism. The threat of capitalism being overwhelmed by state socialism is of course much less than it was before the 1990s. Socialism has become less of a grand design, and more of a series of complaints about capitalism's workings and outcomes – such as inequality. But capitalism never promised to solve all social ills, nor could it: its value lies is the efficient production and distribution of economic goods. And many of the outcomes that are criticised are actually the results of government intervention, not capitalism. Populist politics, with its over-simple diagnoses and prescriptions, have led to a large growth in economic interventionism. We have moved from the idea of state ownership of productive assets to the reality of state control of them. We should not be surprised if such political intervention produces perverse effects.

Creeping control. Even so, regulation keeps on growing. There are many reasons: for example, regulations need government agencies to implement them, and those agencies have a natural interest in expanding their role, typically becoming a major source of new and even more complex regulations. As government becomes a larger and more important economic player, there are more opportunities for rent seeking, cronyism and corruption; and the larger the potential benefits from lobbying. Politicians gain in power, status and privilege, and enjoy imposing their own values on economic and social life – signalling their own virtue to the electorate on whom they depend for re-election.

All this is unfortunate, but even worse is the fact that regulation is almost always counterproductive, precisely because the long-term effects of intervention are so poorly understood and so rarely considered. Minimum wage laws, for example, may seem a positive action against poverty; but in fact they have the opposite effect, by pricing people who may be poor, young and unskilled out of jobs entirely. Or again, regulations that require the lengthy testing of new medicines may well save the public from untried drugs; but equally they deny terminally ill people from taking new ones that might just save their lives. And rent controls may seem to make housing affordable for everyone; but by making it less profitable to rent out property, they cause landlords to take homes and offices off the market or to maintain them less well.

Sadly it is capitalism, not politicians, that is blamed for these consequences – which invariably leads to calls for yet more regulations. Once in place, however, regulations are hard to remove, because they create vested interest groups who depend on them – those enjoying cheap rent-controlled rents, for example, not to mention the regulators who manage the policy. Such expanding, sprawling regulation poses a serious threat to the future of capitalism.

The durability of capitalism

What remains so remarkable about capitalism, however, is its resilience and durability. In one form or another, it has been with us for millennia. As an individualist rather than collectivist social order, it allows individuals to find their own way to deal with whatever social, political or techno-logical realities life hands them. By harnessing the creative genius of each individual, it can survive even the most damaging political interventions: from inept regulations, through misguided economic policies, and even total state planning and control.

Undoubtedly, the politicised version of capitalism that prevails today can be improved on – stripped of politics and state intervention, and set free to work, in its system-atic and all-embracing fashion, for the benefit of everyone. But without something like genuine capitalism, it is hard to see a prosperous and liberal future for the human species.

12 FURTHER READING

Hostile introductions

It is remarkable how many so-called introductions to capitalism are in fact critiques of it, inspired by the historical analysis of Karl Marx.

This is true, for example, of James Fulcher's *Capitalism: A Very Short Introduction* (2004), which shares Marx's fixation with profit, the wage system, exploitation, urban poverty and historical mega-trends, and applies the same thinking to today's fixations on financial instability and globalisation. But it fails to explain what capitalism is, how it actually works or the ideas behind it.

The Wikipedia entry on capitalism (https://en.wikipedia.org/wiki/Capitalism) is a messy work of many authors, again mostly accepting the Marxian viewpoint. It flits from Marxian definitions of capitalism, to their view of its history, to varieties and characteristics of capitalism, on to markets, property and profit, financial capital, monopoly, markets, capitalism and war, types of capitalism again, the role of government and more criticisms, only briefly countered – leaving readers utterly bewildered.

Ha-Joon Chang's *23 Things They Don't Tell You About Capitalism* (2011) is a series of essays, largely suggesting that capitalism is the best of a bad bunch but needs to be controlled and regulated. It suggests that business is short-termist, that globalisation has achieved little, that wealth sticks with the rich, that capitalism is getting less efficient and that free markets do not exist anyway.

Chang's book should be read alongside Tim Worstall's *23 Things We Are Telling You About Capitalism* (2014, http://tinyurl.com/y8fxth82), which counters that politicians are more short-termist still, that protectionism does not work and rests on force, that regulation promotes cronyism and that big governments are far less progressive and flexible than free markets.

Sympathetic introductions

There are also many useful introductions written by supporters of capitalism, who have a better chance of understanding it and explaining it. Perhaps the most influential, and the best place to start, is Milton and Rose Friedman's *Free to Choose* video series and book (1980), which stoutly and engagingly defends a laissez-faire policy of non-intervention, shows the link between freedom and economic progress, and tackles many policy issues such as high taxes, low standards in state schooling and other services, monetary policy and welfare (where the Friedmans propose a negative income tax).

The same authors collaborated on the earlier *Capitalism and Freedom* (1962). Though some of the policy material is dated, concentrating heavily on monetary policy (inflation was then a big issue), there are many useful points on the role of government in creating monopolies, how capitalism reduces discrimination, how regulations benefit providers not the public, and the importance of economic freedom.

Robert Hessen has a short introduction to capitalism in the *Online Library of Economics and Liberty* (http://www .econlib.org/library/Enc/Capitalism.html) which shows how 'capitalism' was invented as a hostile term that still leaves people thinking capitalists want to return us to the dark industrial towns of nineteenth-century England. The supposed remedy – a utopian socialism of agreement and harmony – did not work, so Marx created a 'scientific' socialism, predicting that capitalism would fail. When it thrived, the critics then U-turned to complaining about capitalism's materialism and 'excess'. Sadly, writes Hessen, Westerners do not understand their own system and have been poor at defending it.

A little more philosophical, Jason Brennan's *Why Not Capitalism?* (2014) compares the socialist and capitalist moral case, arguing that the socialist vision is not inherently more virtuous than the capitalist one. On the contrary, capitalism is based on voluntary cooperation, mutual respect and care for others. Unlike socialism, its principles work in large societies as well as small ones. It also protects and grows resources, and allows people to develop and express themselves and to pursue their own vision of utopia.

Arthur Seldon's *Capitalism: A Condensed Version* (2007) is a little dated (being condensed from a 1990 book), but looks at how the Industrial Revolution – contrary to the common view – gave people homes instead of hovels, cheap clothes instead of rags, shorter working hours, better sanitation and many other benefits. It then outlines the rudiments of capitalism, such as property, the price system and customer rights, before showing how welfare, education, healthcare and housing do not need state provision.

In *Capitalism, Democracy, and Ralph's Pretty Good Grocery* (2001), John Mueller explains that capitalism and democracy are neither ideal nor disastrous, but are 'pretty good' at what they do. Though capitalism is said to be based on greed, it in fact rewards honest, fair, civil, compassionate actions. And while democracy is said to be egalitarian and participative, it is in fact chaotic, unequal and apathetic. Between them, they give us freedom, security and prosperity – but not paradise.

Matt Ridley's lecture, *The Case for Free-Market Anti-Capitalism* (2017), points out that free markets are not the same as crony capitalism, corporatism and monopoly. Big firms have made the term 'capitalism' unusable, because they now depend not on economic freedom but on government favours, subsidies, tax breaks and regulations. But economic freedom has halved poverty in twenty years, boosted productivity and generosity, and reduced discrimination and inequality.

Eamonn Butler's *The Best Book on the Market* (2008) is a short guide to how economic individualism works. It shows how markets are never 'perfect' – but how it is the imperfections that motivate everyone within them. Yes, there is market failure: but government failure is even worse.

Exchange raises value; controls kill it. The book covers the resource-steering role of prices and competition, the role of honesty and property, and the morality of the market.

Peter Berger's *The Capitalist Revolution* (1986) shows how capitalism's features – property, capital goods, free markets, automatic asset allocation and a predictable legal system – make it well suited to promote efficiency and progress. It offers a refuge from political power, unlike socialism, which has to be imposed by force – and the grander the socialist vision, the more despotic the rule must be. But capitalism is plagued by viruses, such as the intellectuals whom it creates but who oppose it, and the interest groups who lobby for legal privileges.

The Benevolent Nature of Capitalism (2012) by George Reisman explains why economic and personal freedom are essential to peace, progress and security. Capitalism increases the supply of useful resources, improves the environment, and creates enormous productivity. Prices and interest rates steer investment into the highest-value uses, delivering benefits to non-owners as well as owners. Capitalism is rational, not anarchic, and based on competition – not monopoly.

On capitalism and poverty

There are a number of sympathetic books showing how the spread of capitalism has made a huge impact on poverty. J. P. Floru's *Heavens on Earth* (2013) shows how economic liberalisation in Chile, New Zealand, China and Hong Kong have boosted growth, and helped grow and spread wealth even to the poorest. Tax, regulation and central planning, he concludes, simply prolong poverty.

The Swedish economist Johan Norberg 's *In Defence of Global Capitalism* (2001) is a classic exposition of the positive impact of capitalism and trade on prosperity, education, healthcare, life expectancy, infant survival and much else. Full of facts and figures, it contrasts the performance of neighbouring capitalist and socialist countries (such as Taiwan and China, West and East Germany, South and North Korea) to demonstrate the wide benefits of globalisation and competition. Norberg has updated the argument with his *Progress: Ten Reasons to Look Forward to the Future* (2016), which outlines the post-liberalisation improvements in food quality, sanitation, life expectancy, environment, peace, literacy, freedom and equality.

The Mystery of Capital (2001) by Hernando de Soto Polar shows how capitalism and property rights turn mere unvalued things into productive, valued capital. He notes that while poor people in his native Peru build themselves homes and businesses, these are not useful 'capital' because people have no legal title to the land, nor all the detailed licences needed to trade. He argues that these dead assets can be turned into capital by granting these legal rights – allowing poorer people to have a real stake in the economy, and to develop and prosper.

On philosophy and morality

The Morality of Capitalism (2011), edited by Tom Palmer, is a series of essays by philosophers, writers economists and think-tankers, including two Nobel Laureates (Vernon Smith and Mario Varga Llosa). They argue that trade is a better anti-poverty measure than foreign aid, and that capitalism is highly moral: it is built on trust, not greed; it encourages innovation and value creation; it creates mutual respect and trust; and it promotes and defends cultural values.

The Spirit of Democratic Capitalism (1982) by Michael Novak looks at capitalism in terms of religion and the human spirit. It argues that democratic, pluralist, capitalist societies create caring communities through the clubs, churches, charities and other institutions of civil society. But this essential part of our moral life and completeness is lost when economic and social activity becomes politicised and the authorities take over responsibility.

Ayn Rand's *Capitalism: The Unknown Ideal* (1966) is an eclectic series of essays on a variety of subjects, laying out Rand's robust support for radical capitalism. It roots capitalism in the nature, evolution and rights of humankind; argues that war stems not from capitalism but from statism; bemoans the persecution of big business; discusses markets in broadcasting; reviews patents and copyright forms of property; and argues that capitalism's 'conservative' supporters are suicidally far from understanding, supporting and defending its ideals.

ABOUT THE IEA

The Institute is a research and educational charity (No. CC 235 351), limited by guarantee. Its mission is to improve understanding of the fundamental institutions of a free society by analysing and expounding the role of markets in solving economic and social problems.

The IEA achieves its mission by:

- a high-quality publishing programme
- conferences, seminars, lectures and other events
- outreach to school and college students
- brokering media introductions and appearances

The IEA, which was established in 1955 by the late Sir Antony Fisher, is an educational charity, not a political organisation. It is independent of any political party or group and does not carry on activities intended to affect support for any political party or candidate in any election or referendum, or at any other time. It is financed by sales of publications, conference fees and voluntary donations.

In addition to its main series of publications, the IEA also publishes (jointly with the University of Buckingham), *Economic Affairs*.

The IEA is aided in its work by a distinguished international Academic Advisory Council and an eminent panel of Honorary Fellows. Together with other academics, they review prospective IEA publications, their comments being passed on anonymously to authors. All IEA papers are therefore subject to the same rigorous independent refereeing process as used by leading academic journals.

IEA publications enjoy widespread classroom use and course adoptions in schools and universities. They are also sold throughout the world and often translated/reprinted.

Since 1974 the IEA has helped to create a worldwide network of 100 similar institutions in over 70 countries. They are all independent but share the IEA's mission.

Views expressed in the IEA's publications are those of the authors, not those of the Institute (which has no corporate view), its Managing Trustees, Academic Advisory Council members or senior staff.

Members of the Institute's Academic Advisory Council, Honorary Fellows, Trustees and Staff are listed on the following page.

The Institute gratefully acknowledges financial support for its publications programme and other work from a generous benefaction by the late Professor Ronald Coase.

Other books recently published by the IEA include:

Selfishness, Greed and Capitalism: Debunking Myths about the Free Market
Christopher Snowdon
Hobart Paper 177; ISBN 978-0-255-36677-9; £12.50

Waging the War of Ideas
John Blundell
Occasional Paper 131; ISBN 978-0-255-36684-7; £12.50

Brexit: Directions for Britain Outside the EU
Ralph Buckle, Tim Hewish, John C. Hulsman, Iain Mansfield and
Robert Oulds
Hobart Paperback 178; ISBN 978-0-255-36681-6; £12.50

Flaws and Ceilings – Price Controls and the Damage They Cause
Edited by Christopher Coyne and Rachel Coyne
Hobart Paperback 179; ISBN 978-0-255-36701-1; £12.50

*Scandinavian Unexceptionalism: Culture, Markets and the Failure of
Third-Way Socialism*
Nima Sanandaji
Readings in Political Economy 1; ISBN 978-0-255-36704-2; £10.00

Classical Liberalism – A Primer
Eamonn Butler
Readings in Political Economy 2; ISBN 978-0-255-36707-3; £10.00

Federal Britain: The Case for Decentralisation
Philip Booth
Readings in Political Economy 3; ISBN 978-0-255-36713-4; £10.00

Forever Contemporary: The Economics of Ronald Coase
Edited by Cento Veljanovski
Readings in Political Economy 4; ISBN 978-0-255-36710-3; £15.00

Power Cut? How the EU Is Pulling the Plug on Electricity Markets
Carlo Stagnaro
Hobart Paperback 180; ISBN 978-0-255-36716-5; £10.00

Policy Stability and Economic Growth – Lessons from the Great Recession
John B. Taylor
Readings in Political Economy 5; ISBN 978-0-255-36719-6; £7.50

Breaking Up Is Hard To Do: Britain and Europe's Dysfunctional Relationship
Edited by Patrick Minford and J. R. Shackleton
Hobart Paperback 181; ISBN 978-0-255-36722-6; £15.00

In Focus: The Case for Privatising the BBC
Edited by Philip Booth
Hobart Paperback 182; ISBN 978-0-255-36725-7; £12.50

Islamic Foundations of a Free Society
Edited by Nouh El Harmouzi and Linda Whetstone
Hobart Paperback 183; ISBN 978-0-255-36728-8; £12.50

The Economics of International Development: Foreign Aid versus Freedom for the World's Poor
William Easterly
Readings in Political Economy 6; ISBN 978-0-255-36731-8; £7.50

Taxation, Government Spending and Economic Growth
Edited by Philip Booth
Hobart Paperback 184; ISBN 978-0-255-36734-9; £15.00

Universal Healthcare without the NHS: Towards a Patient-Centred Health System
Kristian Niemietz
Hobart Paperback 185; ISBN 978-0-255-36737-0; £10.00

Sea Change: How Markets and Property Rights Could Transform the Fishing Industry
Edited by Richard Wellings
Readings in Political Economy 7; ISBN 978-0-255-36740-0; £10.00

Working to Rule: The Damaging Economics of UK Employment Regulation
J. R. Shackleton
Hobart Paperback 186; ISBN 978-0-255-36743-1; £15.00

Education, War and Peace: The Surprising Success of Private Schools in War-Torn Countries
James Tooley and David Longfield
ISBN 978-0-255-36746-2; £10.00

Killjoys: A Critique of Paternalism
Christopher Snowdon
ISBN 978-0-255-36749-3; £12.50

Financial Stability without Central Banks
George Selgin, Kevin Dowd and Mathieu Bédard
ISBN 978-0-255-36752-3; £10.00

Against the Grain: Insights from an Economic Contrarian
Paul Ormerod
ISBN 978-0-255-36755-4; £15.00

Other IEA publications

Comprehensive information on other publications and the wider work of the IEA can be found at www.iea.org.uk. To order any publication please see below.

Personal customers

Orders from personal customers should be directed to the IEA:

Clare Rusbridge
IEA
2 Lord North Street
FREEPOST LON10168
London SW1P 3YZ
Tel: 020 7799 8907. Fax: 020 7799 2137
Email: sales@iea.org.uk

Trade customers

All orders from the book trade should be directed to the IEA's distributor:

NBN International (IEA Orders)
Orders Dept.
NBN International
10 Thornbury Road
Plymouth PL6 7PP
Tel: 01752 202301, Fax: 01752 202333
Email: orders@nbninternational.com

IEA subscriptions

The IEA also offers a subscription service to its publications. For a single annual payment (currently £42.00 in the UK), subscribers receive every monograph the IEA publishes. For more information please contact:

Clare Rusbridge
Subscriptions
IEA
2 Lord North Street
FREEPOST LON10168
London SW1P 3YZ
Tel: 020 7799 8907, Fax: 020 7799 2137
Email: crusbridge@iea.org.uk

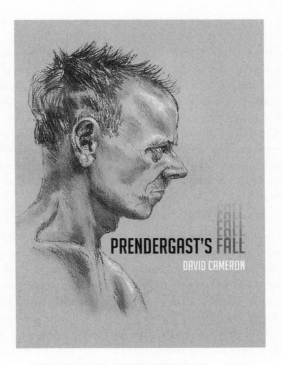

Prendergast's Fall by David Cameron

This is the story of a fall. It won't take a minute.

High up on a ledge, Martin Prendergast sees his life play out before his eyes, but in reverse order. Grim as this sounds, the closer he gets to childhood, the stronger is the sense of possibility.

This two-directional book, which was written to be read from the end to the beginning, can be flipped over and read from the beginning to the end.

It is the work of a writer who has been described as 'one of the most insightful and thought-provoking poets around' (Sunday Herald Books of the Year, 2016).

Published by **Into Books**.

Available to buy now at **intocreative.co.uk/shop**

into books

Rose is good, as is Sufiah. By the time this reaches you, we'll likely be in Greece. They're planning to head to Corfu for a while. They've asked me to join them but as much as I want to see the island, they've got a lot of catching up to do and I could do with a little alone time. Enough drama for one year, thank you very much. An old 'work colleague' of yours has offered me a place for the winter in Montmartre. Very tempted but I'm not sure my savings would keep me going 'til the flowers bloom. Springtime in Paris does appeal. Maybe I could deliver some 'tournesols' on behalf of some old friends. We'll see...

Here's a thought. Am I entitled to holiday pay? Just kidding.

Been doing a lot of reading on my travels, Anaïs Nin, Muriel Spark (thanks Rose!) and of course, a certain Mr Miller. Here's one for you. Do you remember the book that Sonny sent Henry? 'Fools Die on Friday'? I snuck it into my bag for a bit of trashy reading on the way to St. Louis. I figured that no one would mind. Anyway, I eventually got around to it after we'd set sail for Marseille and near the bottom of page 46, there was a stain, the kind made when a cup is placed on paper. Like a coffee ring. So what, I hear you say. It was an old, battered 25c pulp novel, torn, marked and scored. But what if I told you that the ring was around the words 'Against the back of the front seat'? Even Columbo might've missed that one. Probably best not to tell Mr Peterson, eh?

Anyway, just a note to say hi. If I was the kind of girl to display my feelings and emotions, I'd tell you that I couldn't possibly begin to thank you for everything you've done for me over the years. But I'm not, so there. I will continue to write you though, if you'd like...

Keep Elvin away from trouble until I get back and say hi to everyone at The Columbus. Even Miss Washington.

May. x

P.S. And when I do get back, remind me to tell you about an old sailor with a huge, lion-headed dog.'

Chapter 35 - Mail

"No, they were there last week," said Elvin, returning the latest in a short series of postcards to the wall behind the counter. He handed the rest of the mail to Jerry. "Looks like you got one too."

Jerry took the letters, and a cup of coffee, and sat down at the table by the window. Friday lunchtime at The Columbus was over and it was exactly as he'd expected; regulars, office workers and students all with one eye on the weekend ahead. Even though Elvin had started to cover for him, Jerry couldn't bring himself to make plans of his own. Despite his newly appointed assistant manager's protestations, habits formed over decades made it hard for him to stay away from the diner too long. He wasn't cut out for the sedentary life. Maybe he'd rearrange the garage again. Or spend the day with Martin and a couple of beers, casting lines in the shallows on the lake by Turner Road. But first, the mail.

> *"Dear Jerry,*
>
> *How are you and how's things at The Columbus? Miss Washington still busting your chops? Elvin tells me that you're as good as new. Well, almost. The fact that you promoted him to assistant manager suggests that your head might need more attention than those old knees. Haha. Only joking. He's perfect for it. If it keeps his mind off fighting and ... you know ... but please make sure that he's not turning my flat into a gym or a dumping ground. I want to make sure that I've got somewhere to come back to. Mar Saba was an experience and then some. You know me and all that religious stuff, it's never been my thing but...well, just mark me down as a curious undecided for now. We can talk about it more when I get back. When that'll be, I don't know.*

From the corner of her eye, May noticed something moving at the front of the boat. She removed her short-heeled court shoes, a gift from Rose, and clambered up onto the deck for a closer look.